Leading and Managing Schools

Leading and Managing Schools

Edited by
Helen O'Sullivan and
John West-Burnham

Los Angeles | London | New Delhi
Singapore | Washington DC

First published 2011

SAGE Publications Ltd
1 Oliver's Yard
55 City Road
London EC1Y 1SP

SAGE Publications Inc.
2455 Teller Road
Thousand Oaks, California 91320

SAGE Publications India Pvt Ltd
B 1/I 1 Mohan Cooperative Industrial Area
Mathura Road
New Delhi 110 044

SAGE Publications Asia-Pacific Pte Ltd
33 Pekin Street #02-01
Far East Square
Singapore 048763

Library of Congress Control Number: 2010937240

British Library Cataloguing in Publication data

A catalogue record for this book is available from the British Library

ISBN 978-0-85702-395-7
ISBN 978-0-85702-396-4 (pbk)

Typeset by C&M Digitals (P) Ltd, Chennai, India
Printed in Great Britain by CPI Antony Rowe, Chippenham, Wiltshire
Printed on paper from sustainable resources

Contents

The Editors

Helen O'Sullivan coordinates and lectures on the M.Ed course on Educational Leadership and Management in Trinity College Dublin. Her research interests are in the areas of Leadership in Schools, Teacher Professional Development and Professional Learning Communities. Helen's career has included teaching both nationally and internationally, serving as school principal and working as Assistant National Coordinator of Leadership Development for Schools (LDS), Ireland's national agency providing professional development for school leaders.

John West-Burnham is a writer, teacher and consultant in education leadership with a particular interest in leadership learning and development and learning in schools and communities. He has been a school teacher, teacher trainer, education officer and has held posts in five universities. He is Professor of Educational Leadership at St Mary's University College, Twickenham. John is the author or editor of 24 books and he has worked in 24 countries.

Notes on Contributors

Niamh M. Brennan is both a chartered accountant and a chartered director. She holds the Michael MacCormac Professorship of Management and is Academic Director of the Centre for Corporate Governance at University College Dublin.

Tom Collins is the Professor of Education in NUI Maynooth, the former Head of the Department of Adult and Community Education and former Director of Dundalk Institute of Technology.

Paul Conway is a Senior Lecturer and Director of the Cohort PhD in Education in the School of Education, University College Cork. He is a former President of the Educational Studies Association of Ireland (ESAI) and represents ESAI on the Council of the World Education Research Association (WERA).

Rose Dolan is the course leader of the Post-Graduate Diploma in Education in NUI Maynooth. She is a former second level teacher, a founder of Gluais, the youth leadership development programme for second level pupils and a former adult and community development officer.

Paddy Flood was the National Coordinator of Leadership Development for Schools (LDS) and is currently Assistant National Coordinator of the newly formed Professional Development Support Programme for Teachers.

Paula Flynn is conducting research in the area of Special Educational Needs with the School of Education, Trinity College Dublin. Prior to this, she was a post-primary school teacher.

Michael Fullan is Professor Emeritus of the Ontario Institute for Studies in Education of the University of Toronto.

Kathy Hall is Professor and Head of the School of Education at University College Cork. She is interested in cultural perspectives on learning, policy and pedagogy, especially in literacy, and has published widely on these areas.

Jeffrey Lawrence is a principal at Cambridge Leadership Associates. Among his other specialties is leadership development in education. He has done extensive work in the education sector in Ireland, Scotland, the United States and elsewhere.

Marty Linsky is co-founder of Cambridge Leadership Associates, a global leadership development firm (www.cambridge-leadership.com), and a long-time member of the faculty at Harvard's Kennedy School.

Enda McGorman is principal of Mary, Mother of Hope National School, Dublin and an associate member of the Leadership Development for Schools team.

Rosaleen Murphy (School of Education, UCC) was an IRCHSS Government of Ireland Postdoctoral Research Fellow (2003–2005). Her research interests include early childhood education as well as teacher education. She edits *An Leanbh Óg*, the OMEP Ireland Journal of Early Childhood Studies.

Anne Rath worked as a lecturer in the School of Education, UCC from 1996–2009. Her research has focused on reflective learning, transformative learning, critical pedagogy, agency and identity formation, and teaching for social justice. She has published widely on the role of reflective inquiry and portfolios in teacher education.

Michael Shevlin is senior lecturer in special education in Trinity College Dublin and is currently involved in a number of collaborative research projects with colleagues from Ireland and Europe.

Ciaran Sugrue is Reader in Leadership and School Improvement in the Faculty of Education, University of Cambridge. He has been a visiting scholar at the faculty of education in Stanford University and at the International Centre for Educational Change at OISE/ University of Toronto.

Martin Wallace is founding principal of Castletroy College, Limerick. Previously he was principal of St Patrick's Comprehensive, Shannon and has been an associate with Leadership Development for Schools (LDS) since its inception.

Introduction

This book is an analysis and review of the current state of school leadership in Ireland. However, we firmly believe that the issues raised are international in their significance. Each chapter represents a personal perspective and there is no attempt at any sort of collective view. Each chapter focuses on a specific theme and explores it from the author's perspectives of the current issues in education and the implications for the future, particularly with regard to leadership.

The central premise of the book is that both leadership and management in education are important and have the potential to make a significant difference to the effectiveness of schools and the quality of learning and teaching. Moreover, that they have the potential to realise the entitlement of every child and young person to an optimum educational experience so that they realise their potential, however expressed.

To understand the context within which that school leadership must be exercised it is important to consider recent events. Very few countries have undergone the radical social and economic change, within such a short period of time, that Ireland has in the past 25 years. Ireland was a highly homogeneous society with a very clear hegemony around core values. As in many other European countries that is now replaced by heterogeneity and a world modelled on subjectivist approaches.

A number of factors have affected, and been affected by, that change story.

Economic factors

Over time Ireland changed from being an agricultural society with close-knit rural communities to a knowledge society of large urban developments. The dominance of rural life and economic activity was replaced by an urban technological culture. From 1995 to 2008 Ireland's economic success captured the world's imagination and became known as the Celtic Tiger. Ireland became, and can still claim to be, a knowledge-based economy. It became the largest exporter of software in the world and the second largest exporter of pharmaceuticals in Europe after Switzerland. It also became a hub for companies in Life Sciences, Information and Communication Technologies and the digital media space, chosen as a European hub by Intel, Facebook, Yahoo, Merck, Siemens, Microsoft, Pfizer, Apple, Google and Amazon.com to name just a few. Irish self-image underwent major revision with the economic flourishing leading to a sense of confidence and self-efficacy never felt before.

Then came the global financial collapse with devastating consequences in Ireland.

Cultural/societal factors

Historically Ireland might be characterised as a society based on high trust and an explicit social compact. Over recent decades a number of controversies have together led to the breaking of that trust. Like its global counterparts Ireland has suffered the fallout from the economic collapse, and the revelations that attended it, political scandals that rocked the belief in public service for the public good, professionals found guilty of malpractice and finally the discrediting of the church. The fall of the church in Ireland could be described as catastrophic given that for so long it acted not only as the country's moral barometer, but also the guardian of the country's key services of health and education.

The dynamic Irish economy attracted newcomers to the country. Irish society transformed from one that saw emigration as normative to one that enjoyed unprecedented incoming migration. The 2006 census showed that nearly 10 per cent of the population of Ireland were immigrants. While the Economic and Social Research Institute (ESRI) now estimates net outward migration of 70,000 people in 2010, Ireland has been transformed from a monocultural society to a multicultural society within a generation.

The speed of the economic crash and the fall from grace of figures of authority have had the, perhaps, inevitable outcome of a blame culture clamouring for transparency and accountability. The 'social partnership' model of negotiated change, long regarded as a hallmark of the new Ireland with a shared sense of purpose and commitment, is being severely tested.

The collective self-esteem and shared sense of efficacy have been badly damaged. The loss of central and dominant moral clarity may be said to have created a sense of anomie. This may in turn be reflected in a crisis of leadership. Leadership depends on trust; the loss of trust can lead to questioning of the nature and purpose of leaders and leadership in a society. This situation clearly has profound implications for any discussion of the nature and purpose of education.

Education system

During the Irish economic boom, a well-educated, young population was frequently cited by multinationals as one of the factors that influenced their decision to base themselves in Ireland. However, Ireland is facing a very different future and the winds of change are beginning to gather force.

Up to recent times, by one set of criteria the performance of the Irish educational system was deemed a matter for congratulation. The PISA report for 2006 showed that in terms of international comparisons Ireland was 5th in terms of literacy, 14th in science and 16th in mathematics. Thus by one limited and highly specific measure the Irish education system was outperforming those of the UK, Germany and France. Therefore, there was little evidence to suggest that all might not be well. Furthermore in 2009 the OECD confirmed that average educational attainment in Ireland had increased dramatically over two decades. However the results from PISA 2009, published in December 2010, reveal a very different picture. PISA 2009 shows remarkably large declines across literacy (now 17th place in ratings of OECD countries) and mathematics (now 26th place) while science results show Ireland holding a similar position to 2006. When the full cohort of participant countries is taken into account, that means the OECD partner countries, the ratings are more unfavourable still. Analysts caution against reading too much into such a decline. They list a number of factors influencing the outcomes of this international assessment such as changing demographics, increase in the numbers of special needs pupils included in PISA 2009 and the scaling procedures used in PISA itself. However, those reservations notwithstanding, and taking into account the fact that international comparisons are only as useful as the relevance and validity of that which is being compared, and are only as pertinent as the last review, those involved in Irish education have to heed the warnings.

Now questions are being asked, concerns are being raised. In January 2010, reporter Kim Bielenburg stated in a daily newspaper:

> US multinationals have caused some soul-searching among teachers and educators after their severe criticisms of the Irish education system. The American Chamber of Commerce, an influential body that represents some of our biggest employers, believes the school system places too much emphasis on rote learning.
>
> Like many others in the education system, the US employers want more attention paid to problem-solving skills. The US companies highlighted the weaknesses in our Leaving Cert points system. The chamber wants problem-solving capabilities rewarded in exams to encourage the innovation and in a damning critique of the education system, the US bosses criticise the reluctance to make the necessary change to the curriculum to adapt to changing needs.
>
> It says rote learning facilitates high grades in the science, technology and engineering subjects, but this does not reflect the ability of the students to apply their knowledge effectively later in their career.
>
> The attack by the US multinationals comes as another influential body, the Royal Irish Academy, warns of falling standards at third level in Ireland. (*Irish Independent*, 13 January 2010)

Concerns such as those highlighted have been raised internally within the sector by a number of key educationalists in Ireland. The crises of the past two years have led to a radical rethinking of many aspects of life in Ireland. The education system, like many education systems around the world, is being scrutinised as never before. There is a clear need for active leadership, at all levels in the system, if Ireland is to emerge from the current difficulties, economic and societal, with renewed values, renewed trust and a young population educated for a different future. There is an onus on the professionals in education to lead that scrutiny from within with a determination to bring about the changes that are needed. The sorts of questions that might be addressed include the following.

- What kind of society do the Irish people wish to create from the ashes of the recent turmoil?
- What values should underpin education for that society?
- What does the recent Irish story tell us about the Irish education system of the past? What lessons can be learned?

- What should characterise the professionalism of the teacher for the 21st century?

This is a period of great challenge in which many historical certainties are being replaced by ambiguity and choice where previously there was none. We hope that this book will contribute to a professional examination of those choices. Each chapter in the book addresses an area of specific concern and raises questions and possible strategies in order to inform and extend the debate. The book is in three parts. Part One presents a global stance from a generalised 'big picture' perspective on issues of change and governance; Part Two focuses specifically on the Irish context while Part Three looks at the future of school leadership in Ireland, taking into consideration global trends and the challenges facing Irish education. We hope that this is a contribution to a series of informed conversations which in themselves will help to shape the emergent pattern of education in Ireland and in other countries around the world.

We are very grateful to our contributors and to SAGE Publications for their commitment to this project.

Helen O'Sullivan and John West-Burnham

Part I

The Big Picture

Chapter 1

Adaptive Challenges for School Leadership

Marty Linsky and Jeffrey Lawrence

Abstract

The challenges facing education today must be seen in the broader context of the challenges facing society.

The singular reality is that none of us has been here before. Educational leadership will require different behaviours from those we have practised and perfected.

For example, we will spend more time running experiments than solving problems, more time adapting than executing, more time surfacing difficult values choices and orchestrating those conflicts than resolving them, and more time inventing next practices than searching for best practices.

Educational leadership will require becoming expert at working through competing commitments such as autonomy and standardisation or fairness, or accountability and fairness.

To take advantage of these opportunities will require learning new ways and the courage to step out and take responsibility for the future, whatever your place in the system.

Key words/phrases

Educational leadership; adaptive leadership; orchestrate conflict; competing commitments; experimentation; take care of yourself; hunker down; adaptive challenges versus technical problems.

The times we are in

The challenges facing school leadership in the early years of the second decade of the 21st century are intimately entangled with the broader, deeper challenges facing the global community, reaching far beyond the distinctive qualities of education.

We are in a period that feels unique, at least in your life experience, and in ours. The question is whether we are in the midst of a bump in the road or a sea change. Is this an emergency, or a crisis? An emergency is when your house is on fire; a crisis is when it has burned to the ground. An emergency is when you break your leg; a crisis is when you lose it.

Let's look at the times we are in.

Foremost, of course, is the global economic turmoil. Ireland is painfully at the epicentre, still reeling from the bursting of the housing bubble and mourning the long-lost Celtic Tiger. But the world's financial problems are only one element of the strange new world we find ourselves in.

Look at the data.

We are looking at extraordinary environmental and climate challenges. The glaciers are melting. Long-standing patterns of planting and harvesting are changing. There are places on the globe where the shortage of fresh water is an immediate concern. Technology is evolving rapidly. Amazon now reports that they are selling more books for Kindle, their electronic reader, than in hardcover. Five hundred million people are on Facebook.

A by-product of both the technology explosion and the implications of 9/11 is the reality of our interconnectedness. Everything is connected to everything else. Any intervention into the system is going to have consequences, intended or not, in lots of other places.

The Baby Boomer generation is ageing. While the economic problems have slowed retirements, there is a generation and talent gap as those folks born between 1946 and 1965 begin to retire and pass on in large numbers. While they are still around, the sheer number of Baby Boomers will give them a huge influence in society's value choices, including, most pertinently to education, the allocation of public resources. The Millennials, the offspring of those Boomers, are emerging with a very different set of values around issues of privacy, loyalty, and whether work is the centre of life.

The global power structure is rebalancing. US and Western hegemony is giving way to the emergence of new potential superpowers such as China, India and Brazil. Wars are no longer between countries. The challenge to stability comes more and more from loosely or not so loosely connected groups who do not carry a national flag.

In short, we are indisputably in a period of rapid and constant change, greater uncertainty about the future than we have ever experienced, and inadequate information on which to make important choices. This is the context in which the challenges facing education in Ireland exist and in which this book is being written.

In education, as elsewhere, we are living at a time when, as Charles Dickens described a different world in a different era in his opening line of *A Tale of Two Cities*, 'It was the best of times, it was the worst of times'. The central question is whether everyone concerned with the education of our children can seize this crisis as a time for innovation and change, or will continue to hunker down, preserve what they can, and hope that they survive more or less intact whenever things return to 'normal'. The guess here, based on the data we just discussed, is that the new normal will not feel like normality at all, either in its content or its consistency.

So in one sense this is an extraordinary moment to be caring about education. The challenges have never been greater, the opportunities never more present, and the need for success never more critical. All the familiar norms are in play. The authority relationships among the government education agencies, the school administrators, the specialists, the teachers, the students, the parents, private education initiatives, the religious education establishment, and the broader community are all potentially in transition. The good news and the bad news is that there is a public sense of urgency about the global as well as local significance of how we educate our young people that is more palpable than at any time in our memories.

Assumptions about school leadership

If we are going to talk about school leadership in these extraordinary times, let's begin with some assumptions about what we mean by leadership.

First, leadership is a complex but not a technical subject. There are no quick fixes, no easy answers, or, Stephen Covey notwithstanding, no seven quick behavioural changes which will enable you to exercise leadership more often or more effectively than you have in the past. We assume that everyone in the education sector is on the frontiers of leadership.

Second, leadership is an activity, not a person. Leadership is something some people do some of the time. It's a verb, not a noun. No one exercises leadership 24/7. And our assumption is that if everyone reading these words exercised leadership more often than they do, including you, the world in general, and the world of education in particular, would be a better place.

Third, the opportunities to exercise leadership come to each of us, every day, at the family dinner table, in the workplace, in our community and civic lives. And the opportunities come independent of position. Leadership is not the exclusive prerogative of people in positions of authority. Quite to the contrary, some of the most extraordinary leadership has come from people with no formal authority at all (see Gandhi, Nelson Mandela and Martin Luther King, Jr) and people in positions of authority typically do not exercise leadership very much because doing so would put their authority and all the perquisites that go with it at risk. In the education sector, leadership can come from any of the interested factions: teachers, students, administrators, parents, government officials, businesspeople, or electeds.

Fourth, leadership can be learned. The only people we know who think that the capacity for leadership is inherited are those who think they have it. No, leadership is about courage and skill. And both the courage and the skills can be learned. As with young athletes, there may be some people who seem to start out with an advantage, based on how they look or the way they are wired emotionally. But the young athletic phenoms are often not the stars in later years because others have worked really hard to learn and perfect the skills which are necessary for athletic success. Similarly for leadership. Those God-given qualities may provide some people with a head start at developing leadership capacity, but others can easily surpass them by working hard to learn, practise and perfect their own leadership skill set.

What makes school leadership difficult?

We assume that everyone reading these words cares about quality education. And that you would not be reading this book unless there was a gap between your aspirations for education and the current reality. And we also assume that you are looking here for solutions that would be easy to apply or at least steps you could take that would likely make progress without, as the old proverb goes, breaking too many eggs. But leadership in education, as in any other sphere, is difficult work. That is one of the reasons why you – and we – do not exercise leadership more often.

In our view, too much time is spent on the inspirational aspects of leadership and too little time on the perspirational. Here's what makes school leadership so difficult: the most common cause of failure in leadership comes from treating what we call *adaptive challenges* as if they were *technical problems*. What's the difference?

While *technical problems* may be very complex and critically important (such as replacing a faulty heart valve during cardiac surgery), they have known solutions. They can be resolved through the application of authoritative expertise and through the organisation's current values and ways of doing things.

Adaptive challenges can only be addressed through changes in people's values, beliefs, habits and loyalties. Making progress on them requires going far beyond any authoritative expertise and in particular dealing with the resistance that stems from unwillingness to face the losses that will be involved. This resistance makes adaptive leadership dangerous, and therefore rare. Table 1.1 below lays out some differences between technical problems and adaptive challenges.

As Table 1.1 implies, problems do not always come neatly packaged as either 'Technical' or 'Adaptive'. When you take on a new challenge in your education work, whether in a classroom or as an administrator or policymaker, the challenge does not arrive with a big 'T' or 'A' stamped on it. Most problems come mixed, with the technical and adaptive elements intertwined.

Table 1.1 Distinguishing between technical problems and adaptive challenges

Kind of challenge	Problem definition	Solution	Locus of work
Technical	Clear	Clear	Authority
Technical and adaptive	Clear	Requires learning	Authority and stakeholders
Adaptive	Requires learning	Requires learning	Stakeholders

Here's a homey example. At the time of writing, Marty's mother, Ruth, is in good health at age 96. Not a grey hair on her head (although she has dyed a highlight in her hair so that people will know that the black is natural). She lives alone and still drives, even at night. When Marty goes from his home in New York City up to Cambridge, MA to do his teaching at the Kennedy School at Harvard,

Ruth often drives from her apartment in a nearby suburb to have dinner with him.

Some time ago, Marty began noticing new scrapes on her car each time she arrived for their dinner date. Now, one way to look at the issue is that the car needs to be taken to a garage to be repaired. In that sense, this situation has a technical component: the scrapes can be solved by the application of the authoritative expertise found at the garage. But an adaptive challenge is also obviously lurking below the surface. Ruth is the only one of her contemporaries who still drives at all, never mind at night. Doing so is a source of enormous pride (and convenience) for her, as is living alone, not being in a retirement community, and still functioning more or less as an independent person. To stop driving, even just to stop driving at night, would require a huge adjustment from her, an adaptation. (She would have to rely on others, pay for cabs, ask friends to drive her places, use services for the elderly, and so forth.) It would also be a loss, a loss of an important part of the story she tells herself about who she is as a human being, namely, the only 96-year-old person she knows who still drives at night. It would rip out part of her heart, and take away a central element of her identity as an independent woman. Addressing the issue solely as a technical problem would fix the car (although only temporarily, since it is likely that the trips to the garage would come with increasing frequency), but it would not get at the underlying adaptive challenge.

In the corporate world, we have seen adaptive challenges with significant technical aspects arise when companies merge or make significant acquisitions. There are huge technical issues such as merging IT systems and offices. But it is the adaptive elements that threaten success. Each of the previously independent entities must give up some elements of their own cultural DNA, their dearly held habits and values, in order to create a single firm and enable the new arrangement to survive and thrive. We were once called in to help address that phenomenon in an international financial services firm where, several years after the merger, the remnants of each of the legacy companies are still doing business their own way, creating barriers to collaboration, global client servicing, and cost efficiencies. Whenever they get close to changing something important to reflect their one-firmness, the side that feels it is losing something precious in the bargain successfully resists. The implicit deal is pretty clear: you let us keep our entire DNA, and we will let you keep all of yours. They have been able to merge only some of the basic technology and communications systems, which made life easier for everyone without threatening any dearly held values or ways of doing business. In a similar client case, a large US engineering firm functions like a franchise operation. Each of their offices, most of which were acquired, not home grown, goes its own way, although the firm's primary product line has become commoditised and the autonomy that has worked for these smaller offices in the past, and is very much at the heart of how they see themselves, will not enable them to compete on price for large contracts going forward.

We have seen the same commoditisation of previously highly profitable distinctive services also affecting segments of the professional services world such as law firms, where relationship-building has been a core strategy and value and where competing primarily on price is a gut-wrenching reworking of how they see themselves. Yet, as previously relationship-based professions are coping with the adaptive challenge of commoditisation of some of their work, the reverse process is simultaneously going on in many businesses that have been built on a product sales model and mentality.

In an increasingly flat, globalised 21st century world, where innovation occurs so quickly, just having the best product at any moment in time is not a sustainable plan. So, like one of our clients, a leading global technology products company, these companies are trying to adapt, struggling to move from a transaction-based environment, where products are sold, to a relationship-based environment where solutions are offered based on trust and mutual understanding.

The need for making this transformation is stressing many firms, from professional services to insurance to digital hardware. These companies have had great success with an evolving product line, talented salespeople, and brilliant marketing strategies. Now they are finding that the skills required are more interpersonal than technical, both in their relationship with each other within the organisation and in connecting with their customers. A workforce that has been trained and has succeeded in a sales framework is not prepared by experience or skill set to succeed when relationship-building and response is the primary lever for growth. Successful people in the middle third or latter half of their careers are being asked to move away from what they know how to do well and risk their incompetence as they try to respond adaptively to new demands from the client environment.

And in our experience, all of these dynamics are playing themselves out in the education sector as well. We have worked with school systems struggling to make difficult, value-laden choices about which services to children are going to survive and which are going to be sacrificed. We have worked with school principals who are trying to lead change that is experienced as threatening to the professional identity and sense of personal competence of long-time teachers. We have seen small school systems fight to retain some of their identity as they merge with larger systems over the fervent opposition of many in their home communities. We have worked with state governments in the US, who are embarrassed by the test results and drop-out rates of their young people, but are struggling to lead stakeholders into agreeing on a comprehensive strategy for reform that will involve deep change for everyone at the table.

Like Marty and his mother, all human systems, organisations, families, communities, and, yes, educational bureaucracies and schools resist dealing with adaptive challenges because doing so requires changes that partly involve an experience of loss. Ruth is no different from the legacy elements of the newly merged company that do not want to give up what they each experience as their distinctiveness, or the teachers for whom being assessed based on student performance represents a threat to their sense of their own competence honed by decades of experience as valued professionals.

Sometimes, of course, the challenge is way beyond your capacity and you simply cannot do anything about it, hard as you might try. Vesuvius erupts. But even when you might have it within your capacity to respond successfully to the adaptive challenge, sometimes you squander the opportunity and let it slip away. For these cases, we suggest that the common factor generating adaptive failure is resistance to loss.

You know the adage 'People resist change.' It is not really true. People are not stupid. People love change when they know it is a good thing. No one gives back a winning lottery ticket! Everyone who gets married or has a child knows that those life events will bring profound change, but the change is welcomed because people believe those changes will improve their lives. What people resist is not change per se, but loss. When change involves real or potential loss, people hold on to what they have and resist the change. A key to leadership is the diagnostic capacity to find out the kinds of losses at stake in a changing situation, like wealth, status, relevance, community, loyalty, identity and competence. Adaptive leadership almost always puts you in the business of assessing, managing, distributing, and providing contexts for losses that move people through losses to a new place.

Nevertheless, adaptation is a process of conservation as well as loss. Though changes that involve losses are the hard part, most adaptive change is not about change. The question is not only, 'Of all that we care about, what must be given up to survive and thrive going forward?' but also, 'Of all that we care about, what elements are essential and must be preserved into the future or we will lose our core competencies and lose who we are?' A successful adaptation enables an organisation or community to take the best from its traditions, identity and history into the future.

However you ask the questions about adaptive change and the losses they involve, answering them is difficult because it requires making choices and trade-offs, prioritising your values and commitments. That is hard work not because it is intellectually difficult, but because it challenges individuals' and organisations' investments in relationships, competence, and sense of who they are. It requires a modification of the stories they have been telling themselves and the rest of the world about what they believe in, stand for and represent.

Helping individuals, organisations and communities deal with those tough questions, distinguishing the DNA that is essential to conserve from the DNA that must be discarded, and then innovating to create the organisational adaptability to thrive in changing environments is the work of adaptive leadership. In the education arena, the questions about distinguishing what is essential from what is expendable are very much alive. And the losses people fear from adaptations that will meet both the current fiscal constraints and the challenge of providing first-rate educational experiences that best prepare young people for jobs that are needed and available, for rigorous higher education, and for productive lives as engaged citizens and family nurturers are very real. School leadership in the 21st century will not succeed unless people are helped through those difficult choices and the sense of loss.

What are the adaptive challenges facing school leadership?

Education is rife with adaptive challenges, in Ireland and all over the globe. Some existed before the current economic turmoil, some were exacerbated by it, and some were generated – or at least first manifested – by it.

As we have noted above, we believe that adaptive challenges consist of unresolved competing commitments, values and loyalties that keep organisations (or companies, or schools, of families, or countries, for that matter) locked in place. Central to our understanding is the idea of loss. If those competing commitments were resolved, someone or some factions would experience a loss, some values would be left behind or at least subordinated to others.

Some competing commitments are within the education system itself. Some are with other sectors. None are resolvable with technical fixes. So, let's take a look at just a few of the competing commitments that are alive and well in the education sector in Ireland and elsewhere.

Competing commitments 1: *Diminished public resources and multiple legitimate needs v. the imperative to prepare young people for work and citizenship.*

This one is obvious. Every euro spent on education is a euro that is either being taken out of the pockets of already hard-pressed taxpayers or is being taken from some other noble and necessary public purpose, such as safety or infrastructure. Choosing among and prioritising competing claims for public funds is difficult even in times of plenty; it is excruciating in times of scarcity.

Competing commitments 2: *Autonomy v. standardisation.*

Every rule, every regulation, every requirement helps to share best practices and establish objective accountability but undermines teacher and in some cases principal autonomy. Which value is more important to more fully preserve when they come into conflict?

Competing commitments 3: *Community identity v. efficient use of resources and quality education.*

People in Ireland, as in many countries, identify strongly with their communities and having their own school is an important symbol of their unique community. Yet, small schools and undersized classrooms do not give children the quality of education or the breadth of exposure to others' ideas that would occur if smaller schools and school systems were consolidated. Losing a local school is a real community loss, as well as often a significant inconvenience for pupils and parents.

Competing commitments 4: *Accountability v. fairness.*

How do you measure and compare teacher performance across a wide range of situations in a way that is fair; fair to those teachers who have been working in schools for decades and are now facing changes which will challenge their competence and tried and true ways of helping students learn, as well as fair to taxpayers and public officials who need to be better able to assess and measure performance in times of fiscal restraint? And how can we really assess the real impact of a teacher until long after the student leaves the classroom when, of course, so many other factors have contributed to that student's performance as an adult?

Competing commitments 5: *Church-run education v. state responsibility for education.*

When times were good and there were plenty of jobs, no one worried much about whether Ireland was abdicating its responsibility to educate its young people by financing and delegating so much of that to the church-run schools. Church-based schools are a deeply entrenched element of the Irish education system. Just raising the issue of whether the current dual system is fair to all Irish children or is maximising the educational opportunities for everyone, whether or not the church-run schools are providing a superior or inferior experience is, well, political heresy.

What would educational leadership look like in these times?

Given the economic turmoil, the uncertainty about the future, and the rapidity of change, what kinds of new behaviours should characterise educational leadership from wherever it comes: within the sector from government administrators, regulators, superintendents, principals, teachers, parents and students; or outside of the sector from interested citizens, elected and appointed policymakers, or business people?

What would new educational leadership look like in trying to address those unresolved competing commitments listed above or, for that matter, the many other adaptive challenges facing education that anyone reading this could probably add from experience and first-hand knowledge?

Here are some brief thoughts.

(1) *Adapt, don't just execute.* Leadership will increasingly involve sorting through the essential and the expendable, rather than executing a plan. The question people exercising leadership will frequently have to ask is, 'Of all the elements that have got us here, that have helped us achieve what we have accomplished, which are so critical to who we are that they must be preserved, and which, of all that we have valued to date, must we leave behind in order to make progress?'

There is no such thing as a broken system. Any current reality is the product of the conscious and not so conscious decisions of the people in the system. So, when you are trying to change a current reality, you are always threatening a loss to those people and interests who are committed to the way things are.

(2) *Run experiments, don't just solve problems.* In education, as in most sectors, no one has been where we are now. The implication is that no one knows what to do next, but lots of possible hypotheses are out there. Testing those hypotheses suggests leadership will be doing more running of experiments than solving problems. The language of experimentation is very useful. It suggests close monitoring and making mid-course corrections. Lack of success becomes a learning opportunity, not a failure. It also allows for progressive action without all parties having to give up or give in. Learning together is a great way to mobilise deeply divided people (see next item).

(3) *Practise interdependence, not just autonomy.* Internally and externally, the education system needs to forge new relationships, working in a different way with factions that have been on the 'other side' or simply not involved. This might mean everything from more learning collaboration among students, and students teaching younger students, to closer relationships between education and the business community so that both the support for education is wider and deeper and the education system is responsive in its curriculum, training and skill emphasis to the anticipated employment needs of the economy.

(4) *Orchestrate conflict, don't just resolve it.* People in positions of authority are rewarded for solving problems and making decisions. But in the times we are in, what is needed will more often involve orchestrating conflict rather than resolving it. Bringing to the surface difficult issues and then helping people do the work of sorting through those unresolved conflicts of values, creating the holding container for them, rather than always making the decision for them and executing it, will be more of what is required.

(5) *Look for next practices, not just best practices.* Almost everyone in education has access to whatever best practices are out there; the internet has taken care of that. But we are in a period that none of us has experienced before. So while there is always a need for dissemination of best practices and sharing learning, people exercising leadership will have to take the responsibility – and risk – of inventing the future. We caution as well against assuming that something that worked in one locale will work elsewhere. The unique combination and chemistry of factors in your locale suggests 'best practices' are to be considered input at best. Merging inputs in a solution that responds to your situation we think of as creating 'next practices'.

(6) *Take care of yourself, don't just sacrifice your body for the cause.*The education sector in Ireland and elsewhere is characterised by dedicated people who care deeply about their work. Often – too often in our observation – this commitment translates into sacrificing normal human needs. It sometimes feels noble to personally suffer in the interests of what you care so deeply about professionally.

But, from our perspective, leading adaptive change in the times we are in requires you to take care of yourself. Taking care of yourself is not self-indulgence. The world needs you to be at the top of your game. And you cannot be at the top of your game if you have not had a good night's sleep, eaten well, had some exercise and, yes, received the love and affection you need from family and friends to feel like a whole person.

No one else can do that work for you, and no one else will protect the time and space for you to do that work but you. If you care about education, you will care enough to operate at your peak performance level. You owe it to those children.

Chapter 2

Leading System Level Change

Michael Fullan

Abstract

This chapter focuses on 'whole system reform' whereby all schools in the system are involved in improvement. The system is defined as whole states, provinces or countries and whole school districts or regions. System leadership is described at both the school and central levels, in that school leaders have an obligation to work with other schools and entities, and central leaders need to engage leaders at all levels in reform efforts. Specific examples are given in the chapter including a case study of successful large-scale reform in Ontario, Canada. There is a growing interest in how to accomplish success on a countrywide basis. This chapter identifies key leadership issues essential for success.

Key words and phrases

Leadership for change; whole system reform; improving student achievement; managing change; principal as instructional leader.

Paradoxically, leading system change must occur simultaneously at both the bottom and the top of the system. I illustrate this phenomenon of system leadership in this chapter in three ways: one concerns school leaders who become more committed to linking to other schools while still staying in their own principalship; a second involves school leaders who take positions that oversee or otherwise help other schools; the third is system leaders themselves who undertake direct whole system reform. By system I mean all the schools in a district or a state/province or a country. The entire process is driven by the moral imperative of raising the bar and closing the gap in student learning. Moreover, it is based on the actual doing of the work – what I call the moral purpose *realised* (Fullan, 2011).

School leaders broaden their perspective

In the past decade the school principal's role has shifted in all successful jurisdictions from management to instructional leadership or, if you prefer, leadership for teaching and learning. But there is now another equally significant shift in the role. The new role definition of the principal includes the requirement that he or she has the explicit responsibility to learn from other schools as well as to contribute to their betterment. The principals within highly successful districts that we have worked with are expected to – and indeed do – see themselves as responsible for not only their school but also the progress of other schools and the district as a whole. This is their new moral imperative, and the entire system benefits (see Fullan, 2010).

When this outward-facing habit gets ingrained, additional interesting things can happen. One interesting example concerns District 96 in Illinois, USA. This is a small district of 11 schools. The superintendent, and his colleagues, using Professional Learning Communities (PLC) strategies, changed the culture of the district to become a strong learning system, with measurable benefits for all (Dufour et al., 2010). The superintendent, however, took an additional step in order to learn from and with *other* districts. Because District 96 is a small district there are only so many internal resources to draw on, and after a while people begin to want additional connections. After hearing us present the power of 'lateral capacity building' in which peers learn from each other the superintendent came up with an interesting idea. He proposed to his principals that they each link up with a 'sister school' in another district in the region. Some principals were sceptical that it would prove worth the effort but they were willing to try.

This takes the concept of action-oriented moral imperative and extends it into a purposeful, focused learning initiative with a wider but manageable network of schools. It represents a new way of working for incumbent school principals in which they remain as principals but widen the moral net whether this is with schools within their districts or beyond.

School leaders as formal system leaders

The National College for Leadership of Schools and Children's Services (National College) in England formally adopted 'school heads as system leaders' as one of its main themes. The National College is responsible for developing and supporting school heads and leaders of children's services throughout England. Their definition of system leadership is:

> Leaders working within and beyond their individual organisations; sharing and harnessing the best resources that the system can offer to bring about improvement in their own and other organisations; and influencing thinking, policy and practice so as to have a positive impact on the lives and life chances of all children and young people. (National College, 2010)

There are several elements to the programme. One involves the selection and identification of outstanding school principals to the formal status of National Leader of Education (NLE). These leaders are publicly acknowledged and are available on a short- or long-term basis to help schools 'in special measures' (the English designation for failing schools). They are also invited to give input on national policy matters and are consulted on other educational issues.

A similar designation identifies schools that have great track records of improvement and after screening are identified to be National Support Schools (NSS). In the latter case the school head and the whole school staff are engaged by struggling schools on a contractual arrangement to help them improve.

Another cluster involves federations, trusts and academies that work as partners and clusters to improve each other. We recently filmed a primary school federation as part of our motion leadership movie in the UK. The St John/St James federation in Hackney, a borough in inner London, started after one school (St John/St James is a single school) with great school leadership went from special measures to outstanding. When the district contemplated what to do with a second school that was in special measures it was decided that St John/St James should partner the other school with its school head becoming executive head of both schools. The turnaround was so successful that a third and fourth school have been added to the cluster. There is one executive head that runs the cluster, with each of the other three schools having principals who report to her. Teachers and leaders across the schools learn from each other, leaders are moved where they are needed, and leadership mentoring and development is built in.

One doesn't have to follow the English model literally (for more information on these various arrangements and programmes see the National College website, details at the end of this chapter). Any strategy that partners schools, gives people leadership responsibility across the schools, is compatible with these principles of system leadership.

Ontario has a less structured, but equally explicit, programme that enables schools to learn from each other. The strategy is called 'Schools on the Move' in which some 140 schools are identified as having made substantial progress in literacy or numeracy over a three-year period. Schools are profiled on demographics, strategies and results in two pages on the Literacy Numeracy Secretariat's website. Money is made available for other schools to learn from them. Both sets of schools learn. The moral imperative and sense of responsibility to other schools and to the system as a whole is palpable. The point is that school principals and teachers, when the system enables it, and when it is done in a spirit of partnership (i.e. non-punitive), take easily and naturally to this wider system leadership responsibility.

This strong trend of outstanding school leaders taking responsibility beyond their own school is one of the most powerful illustrations of system leaders in action in which those at the school level become the resources to improve the system as a whole.

System leaders

The moral imperative in action at the whole system level is becoming increasingly crucial. Here we are talking about entire states, provinces and countries. A large part of the job of system leaders, of course, is to foster leadership at other levels of the system. They have to develop the policies and strategies, and create the conditions under which the moral imperative does in actuality become realised. This is demanding; they have to get their own state house in order, and then engage the sector in multiple two-way partnerships.

Since at least the turn of the 20th century nations, provinces and states have made the moral imperative more prominent in relation to major reform efforts. You can tell by the titles of the main policy documents and new legislation. In the US we have 'No Child Left Behind', and England had 'Every Child Matters', to cite two prominent examples. The problem has been that there is no focused strategy to realise these great aspirations. In Ontario we have been working precisely on this goal – marrying moral purpose and whole-system strategy – since 2003 (see Fullan, 2010 for a full account).

It is not so much that we invented the ideas in Ontario but rather that we have had the opportunity to put them into practice comprehensively since 2003 when a new government was elected. The Premier, Dalton McGuinty, was deeply committed to the moral imperative of raising the bar and closing the gap for all children; and he was equally committed to implementing a focused strategy to get there. At the starting point in 2003 Ontario's public school system was stagnant. Its two million students and 4,900 schools in 72 districts had been stuck or flatlined in literacy, numeracy and high school graduation for the previous five years. Today, six years later, literacy has moved upwards by 13 per cent and high school graduation rates have climbed from 68 per cent to 79 per cent.

The Ontario success up to this point is based on a set of eight interrelated components:

1 *A small number of ambitious goals*

   The initial focus of the Ontario reform was to improve students' acquisition of literacy and numeracy skills (deeply defined to include higher-order thinking and comprehension) and increase the secondary school graduation rate (including innovations to make programmes more relevant to the life interests of students). These priorities have remained intact since the outset of the reform in 2003. In 2010, a new initiative was added – early learning – which includes the provision of full-day kindergarten for all four- and five-year-olds, beginning with phased implementation in 2010.

2 *A guiding coalition at the top*

   From the beginning, central leadership, especially through the Premier's personal presence, was seen as essential. The Premier chairs a group of leaders that includes the Minister, Deputy Minister, the Chief Student Achievement Officer, the Premier's Special Adviser and other key system leaders. This group, now called the 'Education Results Team', monitors progress, brainstorms programmes and initiatives and helps the system stay the course relative to the core priorities.

3 *High standards and expectations*

   High standards and expectations are implicit in the ambitious targets that were set for students – namely, that (a) by Grade 6, 75 per cent of students would achieve Level 3 or higher on provincial assessments in reading, writing and mathematics; and

(b) within five years of entering high school, 85 per cent of students would graduate. These goals are recognised as 'stretch targets' – as aspirations for the system as well as expected outcomes, representing hefty increases from 54 per cent of students at Level 3 or above in 2003 and 68 per cent graduating from high school in that same year.

4 *Investment in leadership and capacity building related to instruction*

If there is one concept that captures the centrepiece of the Ontario strategy, it is capacity building. Capacity building was first launched by the Ministry of Education with the creation of the Literacy and Numeracy Secretariat (LNS) and the Student Success/Learning to 18 Branch (SS/L18), now coordinated within a new Student Achievement Division. The province has made major investments in personnel (e.g., Student Achievement Officers, Student Success Leaders, School Effectiveness Leads, Student Success Teachers, additional primary and specialist teachers) and resources (e.g., professional learning institutes, webinars, instructional guides). It has also developed finely tuned strategies (e.g., Ontario Focused Intervention Partnerships (OFIP), Schools in the Middle, Differentiated Instruction Professional Learning Strategy, Credit Recovery, Student Voice-SpeakUp) to help improve teaching and learning in Ontario schools.

5 *Mobilising data and effective practices as a strategy for improvement*

When the strategy began, the arm's-length assessment agency, the Education Quality and Accountability Office (EQAO), administered, collected and published annual data on student achievement from provincial assessments; however, few mechanisms existed at that time to integrate this information with other data sources to provide a more complete picture of student achievement. The Ontario Student Information System (OnSIS) was put in place in 2005 to collect and manage individual student records. At the same time, the ministry began to support the development of district school board capacity in data management, data analysis and evidence-informed decision-making, through its Managing Information for Student Achievement (MISA) initiative. LNS also introduced a data query tool, Ontario Statistical Neighbours (OSN), to help both the secretariat and district school boards stimulate improvement and oversee progress. These initiatives enabled system-wide collection of student level data that could be integrated, tracked over time and used to inform policy and practice.

6 *Intervention in a non-punitive manner*

A key feature of the strategy is to encourage risk-taking, learning and sharing of successful practices, while intervening in a non-punitive manner. In other words, the strategy is deliberately 'light on judgment'. Even the turnaround programme for elementary schools (called OFIP) and the School Support Initiative for secondary schools strike a positive tone as they identify schools and district school boards where the data show that a significant number of students are not performing to the provincial standard. Intense support for improvement is provided to these schools and boards in the way of human and financial resources and professional learning opportunities.

7 *Being vigilant about distracters*

From the very beginning, leaders of the Ontario strategy committed to a proactive mindset that 'distracters' would be inevitable but that they would work to minimise their interference with the main priorities. A distracter is anything that takes away energy and focus from the core agenda. For example, ongoing teacher labour strife surrounding annual collective bargaining was a distracter in the period prior to 2003. The government made it a priority to establish four-year collective agreements with all federations and is now in the second cycle of four-year agreements. Other distracters would include ad hoc new priorities and excessive bureaucracy. It is recognised that distracters cannot always be eliminated but that protecting the focus on core priorities is crucial.

8 *Being transparent, relentless and increasingly challenging*

Although the strategy is light on judgment, there are a number of aspects that increase pressure for accountability, including transparency about results and practices, peer interaction and sharing across schools, and negotiation of targets and implementation plans between LNS, SS/L18 and schools/district school boards. More recently, new legislation strengthens the expectation that district school boards (including directors and trustees) have a responsibility to focus on student achievement. More generally, the constant emphasis from the Premier and the government on the core priorities keeps the Ontario strategy in the forefront at all times.

Conclusion

I have spent some time on the Ontario strategy because it is explicit, it has a track record, and it is a great large-scale example of the integration of moral purpose and strategy. The importance of this experience is highlighted by the new interest around the world in whole-system reform. We expect the knowledge and action base in the field of system reform to grow exponentially in the next five years. There is a growing sense of urgency and, equally important, more explicit knowledge about how to achieve system-wide reform. In all cases it will require mobilising leaders at all levels of the system. In all cases it will require focused capacity building of teams and clusters within and across levels. It will require strong two-way partnerships between the 'centre' and the school levels. System leadership is no longer a woolly abstract concept. It is at the heart of achieving deeply embedded reform on a wide scale.

References

Dufour, R., Dufour, R., Eaker, R. and Karhanek, G. (2010) *Raising the Bar, Closing the Gap: Whatever it Takes*. Bloomington, ID: Solution Tree.

Fullan, M. (2008) *The Six Secrets of Change*. San Francisco: Jossey-Bass.

Fullan, M. (2010) *All Systems Go*. Thousand Oaks, CA: Corwin Press.

Fullan, M. (2011) *Moral Imperative Realized*. Thousand Oaks, CA: Corwin Press.

National College for Leadership of Schools and Children's Services (2010) Nottingham, England (http://www.nationalcollege.org.uk/index/about-us/national-college-membership.htm).

Chapter 3

Governance Matters

Niamh M. Brennan

Abstract

This chapter provides insights into the governance of schools from an international perspective where self-governance is promoted. Roles and responsibilities of school boards and school board members are considered, as is the composition of school boards. The elements contributing to effective boards are discussed; in particular the key roles of chairman and school principal which in turn influence board dynamics. Some practical suggestions follow on how to improve school board processes, including agendas, minutes of meetings, board papers, information flows and school board committees. The chapter concludes by referencing the value of school boards evaluating their own effectiveness.

Key words

Governance; school boards; school board members; roles and responsibilities; board effectiveness.

Introduction

At a global level schools governance has been transformed in recent years in response to calls for equity, excellence, accountability and choice (Allen and Plank, 2005). The purpose of this chapter is to provide some insights into the governance of schools, focusing on prior research on school boards appearing in the international education field, with some references to governance from the business/management literature. Interwoven throughout the chapter are practical

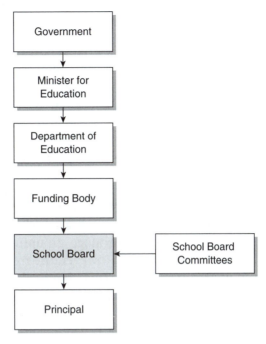

Figure 3.1 Devolution of authority – the school board's position within the hierarchy applicable to a school's governance

suggestions for improving the effectiveness and performance of school boards.

Organisational arrangements for governing schools range from highly centralised and regulated state school systems to models of single school governance with lay involvement (Mintrom, 2001). Local governance is a way of increasing the effectiveness and efficiency of school management while retaining state control. Central to this thinking is the notion that local agents are freed from state bureaucracy which is assumed to reduce efficiency and prevent managers from being responsive to the needs of local stakeholders. In many jurisdictions, the tendency in recent years has been to devolve authority (along the lines illustrated in Figure 3.1) for classroom instruction away from state education administrations and towards principals, teachers and parents, with the objective of generating greater operational effectiveness, greater efficiencies leading to improved outcomes (Mintrom, 2001). The assumption is that greater autonomy leads to improved educational outcomes (Bush and Gamage, 2001). Such devolution of authority leads to more decentralised decision making, with parents having greater involvement and parental choice, and teachers being more empowered (Bauch and Goldring, 1998). The process of decentralisation transfers responsibilities to school governors rather than to principals. This has been characterised as representing a move away from producer interests towards consumers, driven by market-led assumptions that the parents know what is best for their children (Bush and Gamage 2001). Decentralisation allows decisions to be made by those closest to the pupils – principals, teachers, parents, community representatives, citizens and even to some extent the pupils themselves.

A self-managed school is defined as one where there has been signifi-cant and constant decentralisation to the school level to make deci-sions concerning the allocation of resources (Caldwell and Spinks, 1988). International research generally shows support for self-governed schools systems (Bush and Gamage, 2001). The degree to which Irish schools may be deemed to be self-governing is debatable given the centralised administrative system, patronage groupings and funding structures within which they operate. However, the trend internation-ally is towards self-governing schools. This chapter focuses on gover-nance practices when responsibility has been devolved to school boards. School board governance practices ideally should be developed by reference to educational purposes and values rather than discon-nected from them.

This form of decentralisation allows for greater shared responsibility, creating opportunities for greater responsiveness at local level, but with the risk that relevant individuals will not take appropriate

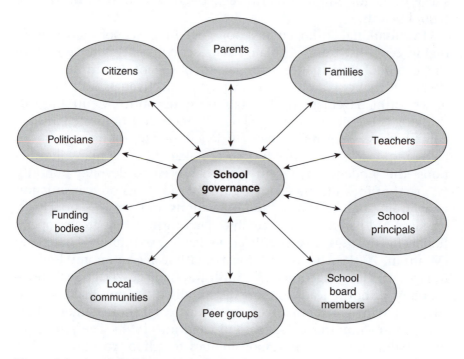

Figure 3.2   A stakeholder model of school governance

responsibility for the school (Allen and Mintrom, 2010). Examples abound of problematic school boards. The model of decentralised governance involves distributed responsibility amongst various groups, and collective responsibility at school board level (Allen and Mintrom, 2010). Figure 3.2 summarises the range of stakeholders over which responsibility may be distributed. However, distributed responsibility brings with it risks, including limitations on the level of control individuals have in exercising their responsibilities. Decentralisation can blur lines of accountability such that it may not be clear who is in control when governance is shared among different individuals and groups (Allen and Mintrom, 2010). Those in control can end up being held responsible for the consequences of their actions when, in a school's governance context, the people assuming responsibility may not have complete control and may not be completely autonomous.

Roles and responsibilities of school boards and school board members

Self-managed schools are governed by boards of trustees/governors/management comprising the principal, staff representatives, parent representatives (one of whom usually acts as chairperson) and representatives of third parties. For the purpose of this chapter, the term board member will be used to refer to trustees/governors/members of school boards. Arguably, the fundamental role of school boards is to improve the educational achievements of pupils (Land, 2002). School board members can exercise considerable influence in the framing and implementation of educational policies. In this model of lay governance, school boards may have considerable discretion to control the management and governance of the school as they see fit. These responsibilities may include the hiring and performance appraisal of the school principal, who is in effect the chief executive officer (CEO). Clark (2000) observes that principals do not always see themselves as CEOs, identifying themselves primarily as professional leaders rather than as managers. Key questions for which there may not be clear answers are: Who are the responsible school board members? To whom are school board members accountable? For what are school board members responsible (Allen and Mintrom, 2010)?

Key roles of the school board

The topics addressed by school boards are extensive and include curriculum issues, performance measures, school governance structures, school property (acquisitions, maintenance and repairs), finance, human resources, industrial relations, legal. For complete clarity, roles and responsibilities should be agreed and documented in a school board terms of reference document. Campbell and Greene (1994) summarise the key roles of school boards as:

- establishment of long-term vision for the school (in Chapter 10 of this volume, McGorman discusses the role of a school board and principal in devising and implementing the mission of a school);
- adoption of an organisational structure including employment of the principal, adoption of an annual budget, adoption of governance policies;
- establishment of systems and processes to ensure accountability to stakeholders, including financial accountability, accountability for course and pupil outcomes and for staff;
- advocacy on behalf of the school and its pupils.

The role of school boards can be categorised between strategy, monitoring (Land, 2002) and support and wise counsel. In this respect, six roles are identified as follows:

Policy setting and strategic planning

  (i) to establish at a high level educational purposes and values;
  (ii) to develop policy;

Monitoring (procedural, compliance based)

School boards have oversight responsibilities as follows:

  (iii) to evaluate the performance of the principal;
  (iv) to monitor the quality of teaching and learning;
  (v) to monitor pupil achievement;

Support

  (vi) to support the principal and provide mentoring, particularly by the chairperson.

McGorman and Wallace in Chapter 10 of this volume discuss the role of a school board in devising an equitable admissions/enrolment policy for a school.

In a business context, boards can suffer from a lack of understanding of the distinction between management and governance. Given the range of issues facing schools, Bush and Gamage (2001) acknowledge the greater difficulties in this demarcation in the governance roles versus the day-to-day roles of senior school professional staff. Clark (2000) teases out the issues between policy and management of schools, observing that the relationship between school boards and principals is a 'flawed' relationship.

Roles of school board members

Some of the prior literature expresses responsibilities by reference to pupils rather than the more holistic school-as-a-whole perspective (for example, Allen and Mintrom, 2010). However, ideally, board members owe their duties to the school as a whole, and not to any individual stakeholder group. This more holistic perspective encourages a longer-term sustainable approach that is in the interests of both current pupils and those that will enrol in the future. Broadly speaking, two duties underpin the proper execution of school board roles by school board members: (i) fiduciary duties and (ii) duties of due care, skill and diligence. Firstly, it is important to recognise that school board members act in a fiduciary capacity, as trustees to act in the best interests of the school. This means that school board members should not act (or be perceived to act) in their own personal interests in a manner that is personally beneficial. Thus, parental representatives on school boards have to be careful not to take any steps which could create the perception that they are acting to promote their own, or their children's, welfare rather than the welfare of the school as a whole. Allen and Mintrom (2010: 443) touch on this when they state:

> … parents seeking to … promote the best interest of their own children might inadvertently generate harmful effects for other children.

The second duty underpinning the proper execution of school board roles is the exercise of due care, skill and diligence on the part of each individual school board member. The exercise of due care, skill and diligence does not require continuous attention by non-executive school board members. Attendance at monthly or quarterly school board meetings should be sufficient. School board members are not (and should not be) constantly in attendance at the school, as this risks interfering with the day-to-day management that is not the responsibility of non-executive board members.

It is important that school board members understand that they owe their duties to the school no matter how they are appointed to the school board, and no matter what group they represent. School board members should also understand that, although school boards are collectively responsible for their decisions, individual school board members are responsible for their individual actions notwithstanding the collective responsibility of the school board. Thus, on occasion, there may be a tension between collective responsibility and individual accountability. In order to ensure there is a common understanding of these responsibilities and accountabilities, the school board should have written terms of reference.

However, the stakeholder model applicable to school governance may suggest that responsibilities of school boards are owed beyond the school itself and include broader public interest objectives. On occasion, there may be conflicts between responsibilities under a wider stakeholder model of governance versus a more focused individual school-orientated perspective. Allen and Mintrom (2010: 444) acknowledge that

> ... recognising the need for balance between the greater good and the good of the individual have long informed arrangements for school governance.

Mintrom (2009: 335) provides an example illustrating how interest group politics can generate harmful outcomes for schools and their pupils, whereby a school board (comprising elected local representatives) was more interested in the role of the board in providing local employment than in its role in educating pupils. Tensions may also arise in the balance of power between lay parental board members and professional board members and this depends on interpersonal relationships, mediated by effective chairpersons and principals (Bush and Gamage, 2001).

Mountford (2004) acknowledges the unrewarded nature of school board membership against the responsibilities executed by board members and examines the various motivations of those holding such positions. She extends this discussion by considering the exercise of power at school board level, and she considers the implications of her findings for school board member–principal relationships with a view to improving these relationships. Lay school board members are unlikely to have first-hand experience of the tasks and activities over which they are governing. In addition, they may not fully understand their governance roles. For these reasons, schools should have proper induction processes for school board members, to help them understand their roles and the complexities of school management.

Composition of school boards

The shift to self-governance for schools depends critically on appropriate people to take on the roles of chairperson and school board members and on their ability to execute their responsibilities effectively. The composition of school boards varies across jurisdictions. Boards generally comprise members appointed by state bodies (for example, local authorities) and possibly by religious bodies, representatives of the teaching staff and members elected by parent bodies. Research has shown that parents are critical contributors to pupil achievement. Parental involvement has been positively linked to teacher rating of pupil competence, pupil grades and achievement scores (Henderson and Mapp, 2002; Simon, 2004). Parental part-time voluntary lay involvement in school boards is similar to non-executive directors on a corporate board. However, not all part-time lay volunteers can be classified as independent, in that some are representative – of parents, of religious groups, of the local community. These conflicts of interest between duties owed to the school versus perceived duties owed to appointers or electors may result in dysfunctional behaviour. Bush and Gamage (2001) acknowledge that school governance roles are held voluntarily, are not rewarded and there may be difficulties in recruiting and retaining sufficient appropriately qualified people to take on the roles. Flood (2011) also touches on the expertise gap at school board level in Chapter 4. Du Bois et al. (2009) examine whether the composition of Flemish not-for-profit school boards influences the objectives/priorities of the school. Seven categories of objectives/priorities are examined including output (number of pupils graduated, performance of pupils in the university and job markets), pupil satisfaction, job satisfaction of teachers and principals, number of pupils, ideological values, prestige of the school and accessibility. Their research is based on a questionnaire to 170 school board chairpersons. They find that objectives/priorities differ across school boards depending on school board size and composition. They urge policymakers to consider the effect of mandated/prescriptive school board structures and composition on school strategies.

Effective boards, board dynamics and behavioural issues

The importance of the way a school board governs, and not just the decisions it makes, is acknowledged by Campbell and Greene (1994). The way boards govern influences their ability to obtain consensus from stakeholders and to contribute to a positive climate in their schools. Campbell and Greene (1994) advocate the importance of boardmanship in the governance of schools. School boards vary on a continuum between inactive school boards where boards fulfil minimum roles, delegating most responsibilities to professional staff, to proactive school boards where board members want to be involved in all policy matters and even in operational management (Bush and Gamage, 2001). Decentralisation of authority is unlikely to succeed unless capacity for governance exists at a local level (Bush and Gamage, 2001). Such capacity requires proactive chairpersons and principals working to increase the effectiveness of school boards.

Quality of role performance, relationships, task efficiency and effectiveness

Robinson and Ward (2005) evaluated good schools board governance in semi-structured interviews with 32 New Zealand primary school trustees using four board scenarios. They found that three key issues emerge in perceptions of the performance of schools boards:

(i) Good governance is a highly formalised activity where conformity to locally and nationally specified rules and roles is important – good governance involves compliance with standard procedures.

(ii) Good governance involves executing specific tasks in accordance with accepted understandings of internal standards of practice. Good practice is grounded in procedural rules to govern the activities of the school.

(iii) Good governance involves high-quality interpersonal relations and effective communication, including appreciating the work of staff, avoiding conflict and avoiding unpleasant surprises. This is particularly important considering the possible conflicts of interests between principals, staff, parents and lay board members. Robinson and Ward (2005) recognise that there is a trade-off between high levels of interpersonal cordiality and the role of the board concerning accountability, the role of the board (especially the lay board members) to engage in constructive challenge and the role of the board in capacity building.

Arguably school board achievement can only be judged by measures of academic achievement (Land, 2002). McGonagill (1987) points to three barriers to school board effectiveness: role confusion (confused board/staff roles), board fragmentation (board internally divided) and board/staff competition (board members and staff competing for control of policymaking and implementation). He advocates four critical steps in building effective boards: developing trust and keeping lines of communication open; specifying the information needs of the school board; clarifying roles; and, finally, creating mutual accountability.

Role of chairperson

The role of the chairperson of the school board is critical in promoting effective governance practice (Bush and Gamage, 2001). A number of useful guides exist on what it takes to be a good chairperson (Change Partnership, 2004; MERC Partners, 2005; Kakabadse et al., 2006; Forum of Chairpersons of State Sponsored Bodies, 2009). These are mainly from a business context but the principles of chairing a board are consistent for all types of board.

Relationship between chairperson and principal

Bush and Gamage (2001) observe that the success of school boards depends on good working relationships, critically that between the chairperson and principal. MERC Partners (2005) describe this relationship as crucial. Key elements to ensuring that this relationship works are accessibility, in order to facilitate formal and informal exchanges of information, mutual respect, honesty and transparency. The job of principal can be a lonely one, and the chairperson can support the principal and be a mentor and a confidant.

Board interactions

A good attendance by board members contributes to better social chemistry around the board table. According to Sonnenfeld (2002), regular attendance at meetings is the hallmark of a conscientious board member. School board members should only take on the appointment if they have the time to carry out the role (Finkelstein and Mooney, 2003). Non-attendance inhibits board members' ability to contribute to debate, to be involved in decision-making, thus impairing board dynamics. It is also essential that board members come prepared to meetings, and have read their papers in advance. Among the processes advocated by Finkelstein and Mooney (2003) for effective boards are: engagement in constructive conflict, avoidance of destructive conflict, and working together as a team. In turn, these are a function of how board members work together as a group.

Qualifications and training

Arising from the largely voluntary nature of school board membership, board members may lack relevant knowledge, experience and skills to serve effectively on school boards. Robinson et al. (2003) find a mismatch between the requirements of the governance tasks required of school board members and their knowledge and skills. They question whether school board members (especially the lay members) hold appropriate professional backgrounds and tertiary qualifications to allow them to carry out their roles competently. They suggest that training be offered to board members to enhance their execution of their roles and responsibilities.

Communication

In evaluating the communication skills of board members, Finkelstein and Mooney (2003) find an ability to explain oneself, to speak out frankly and to listen to be important. In this respect, important personality traits of effective board members include integrity, the courage to speak up, and being forceful and outspoken. These findings come from the corporate world, and may need some moderation in a voluntary school boards context.

Board processes

Governance is a formal process and formality is essential to its effectiveness. Protocols around school board operations should be clear. For any board to perform effectively, clear written terms of reference are essential. At a minimum, the terms of reference should specify the functions reserved to the school board (that is, not delegated to the principal and teaching staff). Other protocols around the operation of school boards including board committees, appointments and resignations to/from school boards, attendance at meetings, etc. should be included in written terms of reference. Table 3.1 summarises a set of standard headings for a typical school board terms of reference. Examples of board terms of reference documents are readily available on the internet. A selection of these can be used as a basis for drafting terms of reference for individual school boards, appropriately customised for the particular board. School board committees should also have terms of reference setting out clearly their roles and responsibilities.

Hygiene factors

The presence of board decision-making process variables influences the dynamic on school boards. These 'hygiene factors' include board agendas, minutes, written papers for meetings, good information flows and school board committees. Grissom (2010: 601), in examining some of these key components of school 'boards' abilities to function well', found that boards with professional decision practices experience less conflict. This section of the chapter provides some practical

Table 3.1   Contents of typical school board terms of reference

Role of the board
Board and its members
  Chairperson
  Lay members of the board
  Staff representatives on the board
  Principal
  Secretary
  Board committees
    Audit and finance committee
  Appointment of board members
    Nominations by a third party
    Elections of representative board members
  Removal or resignation of board members
    Removal
    Cessation of office
    Attendance at meetings
  Independent professional advice
Business of the board
  Delegation of responsibilities to the principal
  Reserved functions of the board
  Board communications
  Board agenda and papers
Review/evaluation of board performance

guidance on best school board practice. Sources used, and useful practical guides, include Deloitte (2004) and the Institute of Chartered Accountants of Scotland (2010). While these are corporate board focused, much will apply to school boards as the principles of running effective meetings are the same.

Board agendas

Formal board agendas ensure that meetings are planned in advance, and that a schedule exists to discipline meetings, ensuring that they remain focused and do not go on for too long. Responsibility for the agenda rests with the chairperson, assisted by the school board secretary. A good chairperson will ensure that other school board members have opportunities to contribute to shaping the agendas for meetings. The agenda should also be discussed in advance with the principal. Meetings are likely to run more smoothly if the chairperson, principal and other key parties meet in advance to plan the meeting. The agenda should identify the person responsible for each agenda item. The agenda should also clearly indicate those items for which a board paper is being circulated, and those items for verbal update.

Minutes

Minute taking is an art form. Minutes range from highly summarised short documents, solely recording the decisions taken at meetings, to lengthy accounts of 'who said what'. The ideal is somewhere between these two extremes. Good minutes will be action-orientated, containing an action column with the initials of those persons charged with the responsibility to take action to follow up points that arose at the meeting. Ideally, minutes should be written up and circulated shortly after the meeting while it is fresh in the mind. In order to prevent time-wasting during board meetings, the minutes of the previous meeting should be circulated to school board members for comment in advance such that the final version of the minutes can be adopted quickly at the start of the meeting. The principles of good minute taking apply to all boards. However, Nowakowski and First (1989) have conducted an interesting study which reflects these principles in school board context. Pointing out that writing board minutes requires discretion and good judgment, Zinski (2006) has some useful tips including: avoid blow-by-blow accounts; reflect flexibility and judgment in writing minutes; choose between long-form and short-form style minutes and be consistent in the style chosen; in relation to board resolutions, be accurate and get the wording right.

Matters arising

A 'matters arising' schedule should be maintained by the school board secretary, setting out live issues to be addressed in the future. The schedule should indicate which issues are on target/completed, in progress, or overdue. A visual colour coding system might be applied, green indicating issues completed, amber for issues in progress, and red for overdue issues.

Written papers for meetings

A formal board pack should be circulated to school board members well in advance of meetings. In addition to the agenda, minutes and matters arising schedule, the board pack should contain a report from the principal, a finance report, and any other papers dealing with issues on the agenda. Other than in exceptional circumstances, papers should not be tabled at meetings as school board members will not have adequate time to read, digest and consider such papers. Board papers should be accompanied by a statement setting out clearly the purpose of the paper (for example, for decision (identifying precisely the decision requested), for discussion, for noting).

Good information flows

School boards require high-quality information in order to function effectively. Boards face real dangers if information is withheld or if news flows are filtered such that only positive news is allowed through to the board. If there is a failure of information flows the governance system breaks down. Information is a weapon. How many board members have experienced being flooded and over-whelmed with information, which turned out to be irrelevant, with the key data being withheld? Some common information manipulation techniques include the following:

- inadequate, incomplete information – information too costly, time-consuming to obtain;
- information flows to the board tightly scripted;
- concealment of information;
- omitting or trivialising bad news;
- using excessive subtlety to communicate key information such that it is lost on the reader;
- swamping the board with voluminous amounts of information;
- tabling information at board meetings, allowing insufficient time to read the material;
- scheduling trivial matters early in meetings, ensuring critical issues are rushed at the end of meetings;

some of the above insights come from the corporate world, and may need some tempering in a schools board context.

School board committees

An effective means of preventing school board meetings becoming overloaded is to establish committees to assist boards in executing their duties. Such committees are board (not management) committees, and should not interfere with the day-to-day running of the school. A common board committee is a Finance and Audit Committee, whose function is to oversee the financial management of the school on behalf of the board. This means that less school board time is taken up with financial and audit matters, which have already been scrutinised by the Finance and Audit Committee. Members of the Finance and Audit Committee are likely to be the more financially literate school board members. Minutes of the Finance and Audit Committee and any other board committees should be circulated at board meetings, to ensure that all school board members are fully familiar with the work of the committees.

Evaluating school board performance

There is evidence from the literature of variable school board per-formance. It can assist the smooth functioning of boards to evaluate board performance from time to time. Ideally this is facilitated by external independent parties. However, given the financial con-straints applying to most schools, a more pragmatic approach might be a self-valuation process led by the chairperson. A senior school board member might lead the evaluation of the chairperson's per-formance. Danzberger et al. (1987) discuss efforts in the US to provide a framework (what they call 'indicators of effectiveness') for evalua-tion of school boards' and school board members' performance to improve their effectiveness.

Concluding comments

Governance is a multifaceted, multidimensional concept. The duties and responsibilities of those charged with governance are onerous and demanding. School board members act in a voluntary and unremu-nerated capacity. This chapter has attempted to provide some clarity on the roles and responsibilities of governance in a schools context. In addition, some practical advice on hygiene issues is offered. However, ultimately, the success of school boards depends on the interpersonal relationships around the school board table and on the social chemistry of the group. The influence of the chairperson and principal are critical in this respect. Ideally, there should be equitable sharing of power so that all involved are able to make worthwhile contributions to decision making (Clark, 2000). School boards need to be robust, effective social systems (Sonnenfeld, 2002).

References

Allen, A. and Mintrom, M. (2010) 'Responsibility and school governance', *Educational Policy*, 24(3): 439–64.

Allen, A. and Plank, D.N. (2005) 'School board election structure and democratic representation', *Educational Policy*, 19: 510–27.

Bauch, P.A. and Goldring, E.B. (1998) 'Parent-teacher participation in the con-text of school governance', *Peabody Journal of Education*, 73(1): 15–35.

Bush, T. and Gamage, D. (2001) 'Models of self-governance in schools: Australia and the United Kingdom', *International Journal of Education Management*, 15(1): 39–44.

Caldwell, B.J. and Spinks, J.M. (1988) *The Self-Managing School*. London: Falmer Press.

Campbell, D.W. and Greene, D. (1994) 'Defining the leadership role of school boards in the 21st century', *The Phi Delta Kappan*, 75(5): 391–95.

Change Partnership (2004) *What Makes a Great Board Chair?* London: The Change Partnership.

Clark, J. (2000) 'Boards of trustees and school principals: a flawed policy-management relationship', *Directions: Journal of Educational Studies*, 22(1): 85–96.

Danzberger, J.P., Carol, L.N., Cunningham, L.L., Kirst, M.W., McCloud, B.A. and Usdan, M.D. (1987) 'School boards: the forgotten players on the education team', *The Phi Delta Kappan*, 69(1): 53–9.

Deloitte (2004) *Responsibilities of Directors in Ireland*. Dublin: Deloitte.

Du Bois, C., Caers, R., Jegers, M., De Cooman, R., De Gieter, S. and Pepermans, R. (2009) 'The link between board composition and board objectives: an empirical analysis on Flemish non-profit schools', *Managerial and Decision Economics*, 30(3): 173–82.

Finkelstein, S. and Mooney, A.C. (2003) 'Not the usual suspects: how to use board process to make boards better', *Academy of Management Executive*, 17(2): 101–13.

Flood, P. (2011) 'Leading and managing Irish schools', in H. O'Sullivan and J. West-Burnham (eds), *Leading and Managing in Schools*, London: Sage Publications. pp. 43–58.

Forum of Chairpersons of State Sponsored Bodies (2009) *A Chairperson's Guide to Good Governance*. Dublin: Forum of Chairpersons of State Sponsored Bodies.

Grissom, J.A. (2010) 'The determinants of conflict on governing boards in public organizations: the case of California school boards', *Journal of Public Administration Research and Theory*, 20(3): 601–27.

Henderson, A.T. and Mapp, K.L. (2002) *A New Wave of Evidence: The Impact of School, Family and Community Connections on Student Achievements*. Austin, TX: Southwest Educational Development Laboratory.

Institute of Chartered Accountants of Scotland (2010) *Directors. Their Role and Responsibilities in a Private Company*. Edinburgh: Institute of Chartered Accountants of Scotland.

Kakabadse, A., Kakabadse, N.K. and Barratt, R. (2006) 'Chairman and chief executive officer (CEO): that sacred and secret relationship', *Journal of Management Development*, 25(2): 134–50.

Land, D. (2002) 'Local school boards under review: their role and effectiveness in relation to students' academic achievements', *Review of Educational Research*, 72(2): 229–78.

McGonagill, G. (1987) 'Board/staff partnership: the key to the effectiveness of state and local boards', *The Phi Delta Kappan*, 69(1): 65–8.

McGorman, E. and Wallace, M. (2011) 'New schools for new century ', in H. O'Sullivan and J. West-Burnharn (eds), *Leading and Managing Schools*. London: Sage Publications. pp. 141–56.

MERC Partners (2005) *The Art of Chairing a Board. A Survey of Irish Directors by the Change Partnership Ireland*. Dublin: MERC Partners. The Change Partnership Ireland.

Mintrom, M. (2001) 'Educational governance and democratic practice', *Educational Policy*, 5(5): 615–43.

Mintrom, M. (2009) 'Promoting local democracy in education: challenges and prospects', *Educational Policy*, 23(2): 329–54.

Mountford, M. (2004) 'Motives and power of school board members: implications for school board–superintendent relationships', *Educational Administration Quarterly*, 40(5): 704–41.

Nowakowski, J. and First, P.F. (1989) 'A study of school board minutes: records of reform', *Educational Evaluation and Policy Analysis*, 11(4): 389–404.

Robinson, V. and Ward, L. (2005) 'Lay governance in New Zealand's schools: an educational, democratic or managerialist activity?', *Journal of Educational Administration*, 43(2): 170–86.

Robinson, V.M.J., Ward, L. and Timperely, H. (2003) 'The difficulties of school governance: a layperson's job?', *Educational Management and Administration*, 31(3): 182–263.

Simon, B.S. (2004) 'High school outreach and family involvement', *Social Psychology of Education*, 7(2): 185–209.

Sonnenfeld, J.A. (2002) 'What makes great boards great', *Harvard Business Review*, September 2002.

Wallace, M. (2011) 'New schools for a new century', in H. O'Sullivan and J. West-Burnham (eds), *Leading and Managing in Schools*, London: Sage Publications. pp. 141–56.

Zinski, C.J. (2006) 'Choose your words carefully: board minutes matter', *American Bankers Association Banking Journal*, 98(10): 22–32.

Acknowledgement: This chapter was written during a Research Performance Panel Visit to the University of South Australia Centre of Accounting, Governance and Sustainability, for whose support I am grateful.

Part II

The Irish Picture

Chapter 4

Leading and Managing Irish schools: A Historical Perspective

Paddy Flood

Abstract

This chapter tracks the trajectory of the evolving role of school leaders in Irish primary and post-primary schools. The leadership role of the principal teacher is seen as emerging and incomplete. Set against the backdrop of a recent OECD study, *Improving School Leadership*, the chapter identifies implications for policy and practice if the key role of the principal teacher in improving learning and teaching is to be optimised. This implies a movement from traditional views of the role, the freedom of school leaders to make more decisions at school level and a willingness by principals and teachers to engage further in self-evaluation and feedback. The lack of interest in leadership positions and the demanding managerial aspects of the principal's role are portrayed as significant challenges in the task of improving the impact of school leadership, while continuous leadership development that supports a focus on learning and teaching is identified as an important lever in improving school quality.

Key words

Leadership development; managerialism; principal; traditional; management; administration; learning-centred; learning; teaching.

Introduction

The past three decades have witnessed a particularly rapid period of change and transformation in Irish society. During this period the economy has experienced accelerated growth followed by an equally rapid decline, the role of the church in society has been greatly diminished, immigration and emigration sit side by side, liberal legislation has granted significant rights to minority groups and the dominance of agriculture as an economic force has been somewhat replaced by technological and scientific industries. Schools have experienced a correspondingly intense period of change and development.

The legislative context of schooling is accounted for in the Education Act 1998 and subsequent acts including the Educational Welfare Act and the Education of Persons with Special Educational Needs Act 2004. The challenge of developing schooling that is fit for purpose in a new economic and technological landscape is of strategic importance to Ireland. Schools also have to adjust to the new social reality of 21st century Ireland where the profile of the family, of the student and of community has changed dramatically. English as a first language for pupils can no longer be taken for granted, pupils with special educational needs are often found in mainstream schools, and technology has begun to impact on the teaching and learning agenda. The education system has expected much of Irish schools in terms of curriculum change, a move towards collaborative planning, greater accountability, more involvement of parents and community, and an ability to integrate pupils from diverse backgrounds and circumstances.

To a large extent, schools deal pragmatically with challenges as they arise, and Irish schools have done so without causing any real public concerns about the quality of education. This is not an insignificant achievement, given the manner in which the quality of education raises public concerns in some other countries. Certainly the policies, practices and methodologies drawn upon by schools have been challenged to modernise and change. It is within this context of change, ambiguity, opportunity and uncertainty that school leaders have led teachers, parents, pupils and school communities. The context of schools (and school sectors) may differ, but the underlying reality is that the role of the principal teacher, and to a lesser extent the deputy principal, has shifted significantly. Today there is an acknowledgement of the leadership role of the principal compared to the administrative nature of the role as it was up to the early 1970s. However, amid role expansion and intensification there is a real sense of drift and ambiguity as to the moral and primary focus of the role of school principal. This chapter seeks to trace the emerging professional identity, practices and potential of school leaders in Irish education and to make a number of observations on how school leaders might offer the best possible leverage in improving Irish education in future years. The chapter will explore the leverage school leadership offers education, will examine the impact of the past on current practices and will suggest ways in which the leverage of school leaders to impact on learning and teaching can be enhanced into the future.

Leadership and leverage

The need for a clearer focus on the role of the Irish primary principal was documented by Fullan (2006: 13)

> My first conclusion, at this juncture in the Irish Education Reform agenda, is that the principalship needs serious attention that it has not yet received. The time is right to change this and to follow through with action that will strengthen the role and impact principals can have in school improvement in the 21st century.

Any discussion around the reform of school leadership can be usefully set against what we know about the potential of school leadership to improve the quality of teaching and learning. An initial observation on the impact of school leadership is that it cannot achieve much on its own. Leadership is an indirect activity, whereby those who lead, while sometimes delivering the service on the front line, are primarily charged with creating the circumstances and context in which learning and student growth can take place (Hallinger and Heck, 1998). This focus on learning and teaching is strengthened by McKinsey and Company (2007) who, when reporting on the common factors in some of the world's most successful education systems, identified teacher quality as the single most influential factor in raising student outcomes. In particular McKinsey suggests that the best education systems concentrate on:

- getting the right people to become teachers;
- developing them into the best instructors they can be;
- ensuring that the system is able to deliver the best possible instruction for each child.

McKinsey's findings challenge school leadership policy and practice to focus on assisting the development of teachers into the best instructors they can be, and to create the optimum opportunities for learning for each child in Irish schools. Elmore (2008, Vol. 2) contends that leadership is the improvement of practice while the National College of School Leadership (NCSL) (2006) links high-performing schools with high-performing leaders. This notion of learning-centred leadership has come to the fore in recent decades. School leaders are often the bridge between policy and practice, and policy initiatives are unlikely to succeed unless there is a sense of ownership and commitment among school leaders (OECD, 2008, Vol. 2). Amid continued discourse on the ideal role of school leaders in Irish schools, there appears to be a real challenge in creating the conditions where leaders can focus on learning and teaching. Learning-centred leadership activities include:

- leading by example, particularly through interacting with students in classrooms;
- monitoring students' achievements, progress and the quality of teaching;
- using data to analyse and evaluate performance;
- generating and sustaining discussions about teaching and learning;
- sustaining school improvement;
- creating structures and school conditions to sustain these activities.
  (NCSL, 2006: 20)

Having practised as a school leader and having engaged in leadership development for the past 15 years, I find that some aspects of learning-centred leadership remain culturally and practically challenging (if not uncomfortable) in the Irish context. Some of the activities listed above can evoke a sense of taboo in Irish schools. Direct monitoring of teaching and evaluation of performance are particularly foreign to the culture of our schools. Symptomatic of this is the fact that the induction process for primary teachers is conducted by the inspectorate, an external agency, as opposed to the school and the school leader. It is difficult to envisage how a greater involvement of school leaders in the learning process can be truly realised without leaders observing, and discussing, practice on the site of learning, the classroom. In essence, the scope of school leaders to impact on learning and teaching remains hostage to traditions and practices that have developed over a century. A continued challenge for school principals, and for our education system, is the ability to abandon those practices that are obsolete. Correspondingly, in the light of change and new evidence, they are challenged to embrace new practices, however uncomfortable, if these changes can be seen to be of ultimate benefit for student learning.

School leadership: a core concern

Sachs (2001) outlines the shifting sands of professional identity in contemporary service provision. The nature of professional work is often headed in the direction of 'managerialism', where school leaders implement policies and directives that are externally devised. A competing, more active, 'democratic' model of professionalism offers the individual the opportunity to create the agenda and to be a transformer of practice.

This tension has been highlighted in Ireland in recent years. A dominant trend at school leaders' conferences in Ireland has been a yearning for more autonomy for school leaders to make decisions and to allocate resources as they see fit in the context of the individual school. Equally school leaders bemoan the level of paperwork, form filling and bureaucracy associated with the job (Morgan and Sugrue, 2005). Fullan's call for serious attention to be given to the role of school principal is centred on these tensions. Clive Byrne, National Association of Principals and Deputy Principals (NAPD) (2009), articulates the need for a more learning-centred approach to school leadership and also expresses frustrations of his members:

> The current administrative workload severely limits their capacity to have any ongoing role in influencing student learning. (Byrne, 2009: 130)

He proceeds to espouse a different vision for the professional activity of school leaders, if freed from the administrative workload that he suggests:

> At second level, funds must be provided to enable the school Principal and Deputy Principal to be the leaders of learning in their schools. (Byrne, 2009: 130)

The current reality in Ireland appears to suggest that school leaders do not line up in philosophically opposed camps in relation to where they see themselves as professionals. School leaders, rather, adopt what Moore et al. (2002) noted as strategic pragmatism in the manner in which they embrace their role. In the current Irish context one suspects that Irish school leaders acknowledge the public appetite for accountability and transparency while also seeking to be more creative and more proactive in addressing the learning and teaching challenges that face schools.

School leaders enter the role to make a difference (Morgan and Sugrue, 2005). They seek out opportunities to impact on the lives of pupils and, as previously mentioned, it is important that they have ownership in the change process. Professional fulfilment for school leaders into the future necessitates continuing, and improved, scope for principals and other leaders to be agents of change at school level; change that improves practice. OECD (2008, Vol. 1) suggests that in order for this to happen four distinct sets of policy considerations will have to be explored:

- further clarification of the role of school leaders;
- distribution of school leadership;
- improved development of school leaders;
- enhancing the attractiveness of the leadership role.

The origins of Irish school leadership

Coolahan (1981: 141) notes that:

> factors in Irish modern history such as the colonial past, the religious affiliation of the population, the cultural traditions of the people, the economic structure and the goals set for education have all shaped the unusual, interesting and complex structure of the present-day education system.

A fuller appreciation of the current context of Irish school leadership can be extrapolated from a closer scrutiny of the evolution of leadership roles in Irish education. The term 'school leadership' is a most recent arrival on the educational landscape. One principal of long standing once remarked to me: 'Let me get on with the job and steer well clear of that leadership stuff'.

Leadership has been described as a process of influence, where one can enlist the support of others in pursuit of a common task. It is an agenda-setting activity. It requires authority, resources, acknowledged pathways to influence, and the scope to create a change agenda. The history of Irish education is characterised by a tension and partnership between the church, who own the majority of schools, and the state, which funds and aids schools. This partnership set the agenda and at various times sought to micro-manage the operations of schools, leaving few avenues of influence open to the principal teacher.

This sharing of power between church and state was described by the OECD as an arrangement 'that arose and had been conserved through force of circumstance' (1991: 37); circumstances alluded to by Coolahan above.

Furthermore, amidst the church–state control of education, Irish teacher trade unions developed significant power and influence in the education system. The role of the principal teacher before 1970 was an administrative one, coupled with an expectation of moral leadership for the school and the community. Decisions and directives came from the state or the church, depending on the nature of the issue at hand, and were ameliorated through the trade union interpretation. Teachers taught the curriculum laid down by the state, were loyal to the ethos as shaped by the church and were inspected by departmental inspectors. There was little scope for principal influence in this environment. The lack of scope for leadership is also further due to the fact that from the birth of the state until the 1960s Irish education had been 'both static and gravely under-resourced', as it was bluntly described by OECD (1991: 25). In such an educational landscape as described above school principals had neither the power, the resources, the support nor the autonomy to significantly influence change in schools. Neither was it expected of them to do so.

The 1960s and early 1970s proved to be a relatively dynamic period in Irish education, particularly at post-primary level with the arrival of free education, school transport and the emergence of a new model of schools (Community and Comprehensive) to provide education in areas that previously had no access to post-primary education. At primary level a new curriculum was introduced (1972) and in 1973 the Department of Education developed a circular outlining the responsibilities and authority of the Irish primary principal. In 1975 Boards of Management were introduced to primary schools. The 1970s and 1980s can be characterised as a period of incubation for school leadership. The term 'management' became the dominant descriptor of the principal's role; a role which the Irish National Teachers' Organisation (INTO) (1991) noted had changed substantially over a 20-year period. The INTO review pointed to the fact that school principals had assumed a responsibility for whole-school planning and implementation of initiatives while becoming more centrally involved in managing teachers, liaising with parents and developing links with the community. In this environment appointing 'a safe pair of hands' became orthodox practice (Sugrue, 2003). By 1991 the OECD was moved to observe that the role of the principal teacher in making decisions, resource management, developing interpersonal and community relations had become more widespread in schools and that this necessitated training for principal teachers and others in positions of senior responsibility. A stratum of middle management positions in larger schools was also advocated to support the growing role of the principal teacher. However, while there was a call for a greater investment in school management and school leaders, the same report suggests that the scope and influence of principal teachers in Ireland was unlikely to grow significantly. In particular OECD concluded that the independence of teachers in their own practice was uncontested.

In the light of the discourse on the professional identity of school leaders it is reasonable to assume that the period from the mid 1960s to the early 1990s was one where the managerial responsibilities of school leaders grew significantly, but the influence of the principal teacher on the content and methodologies of classroom teaching and learning throughout the school remained a relative 'no-fly zone'.

An evolving leadership era

If the period from 1921 to the 1960s was 'static' and under-resourced, the era from the mid 1990s to today was one of intense, relentless societal and educational change. It was also a period in which the traditional religious principal teacher was increasingly replaced with a lay leader, often with a new style of leadership. Globally the potential of school leadership to transform and improve schools became recognised, and national governments acknowledged the evidence that school leaders have a pivotal role to play in leading schools through less certain, faster-changing times. An emerging confidence among school leaders, coupled with the need for practitioners to network in order to meet the increasingly challenging demands of the role, led principal teachers and deputy principals to come together under the auspices of the National Association of Principals and Deputy Principals (NAPD) and Irish Primary Principals Network (IPPN). Both organisations injected new urgency and vigour into the leadership agenda and fostered an increased sense of professional collegiality and identity among school leaders. National conferences and other events gave leaders access to a wider range of thinking on how schools can deliver on the moral imperative of improving schools. This new interest in school leadership is also reflected in the increasing attention paid to school leaders by other stakeholders including management bodies, trade unions and trust bodies. The principals' professional associations were adamant that, in order for principals to realise their potential in the education system, a national initiative in developing school leaders should be introduced. The Leadership Development for Schools Programme (LDS) was perhaps a defining landmark in terms of the increased professional recognition afforded to school leaders at this time. The initial work of LDS concentrated on profiling school leadership in 2002. This collaborative process involving all relevant stakeholders was a formal acknowledgement that school leadership was a distinct professional endeavour which required competences, skills, knowledge and an ability to engage in practices that maximised the contribution of schools to pupil growth and development.

The Leadership Development for Schools' (LDS) *School Leadership – A Profile* (2002) became a reference point for the professional development needs of school leaders and outlined the complexity of school leadership. This led to the introduction of new professional development initiatives for school leaders including *Misneach*, an induction programme for newly appointed principals, *Tánaiste* for newly appointed deputy principals, *Forbairt* for established principals and deputy principals, and more recently *Tóraíocht*, a postgraduate programme for aspiring school leaders. These were supplemented by a range of tailored courses and programmes for leaders in special schools and disadvantaged schools. Support in establishing a collaborative school development planning process in schools was introduced, bringing more staff members into contact with leadership opportunities. A new era of active school leadership was heralded in, characterised by the pursuit of a relentless improvement agenda, rapid response to social change and the establishment of schooling on a legislative footing.

Notwithstanding this new era where principals are more dynamic, or overworked (depending on one's perspective) traditional perceptions of the role remain strong. While the work undertaken and improvements led by school leaders are acknowledged, the level of direction by the state remains high. The level of autonomy afforded to school leaders in Ireland, while higher than in some Western countries, remains significantly lower than in others (OECD, 2008, Vol. 1). The result is that school leaders have low levels of flexibility in relation to the spending of certain grants, the organisation of special needs education, and the structure of the school timetable and the evaluation of teacher performance.

At national level the professional associations for school leaders gained significant initial influence through working with departmental bodies and others, yet remain unrepresented at a number of strategically important national forums. In addition to this, the image of school leadership as portrayed in the media and in public discourse is often heroic, but quite negative in terms of the workload, attractiveness and scope for making a real difference. In conclusion while the past decade, in particular, has heralded a much more robust, active, reforming model of school leadership in response to intense change, the potential of school leadership to assist in further transforming Irish education remains unfulfilled.

Improving Irish school leadership

The remainder of this chapter focuses on how the improvement of practices in Irish schools can be enhanced through the improvement of school leadership. It draws heavily on the OECD's recommendations, *Improving School Leadership* (OECD, 2008, Vol. 1) as set against the Irish experience outlined in the Irish Country Background Report (LDS, 2007). Recognition of context and of a complex past is the starting point for future exploration of Irish school leadership.

Clarity of purpose

OECD (2008, Vol. 1) espouses the notion of clarity of purpose for school leadership broadly in line with the notion of learning-centred leadership activities detailed by NCSL (2004). It challenges the idea that school leaders can be all things to all people and yet be clear in pursuing an agenda that focuses on school improvement. The Irish Country Background Report by LDS (2007) clearly questions the sustainability of the current Irish situation in a similar manner to Fullan (2006). In particular, the structure of Irish education conveys significant and complex responsibilities to the Board of Management of schools at local level. These require a significant leadership impact by boards. Yet, boards appear to be hostages to the level of expertise of board members, notwithstanding any support received from parent bodies and others. Principal teachers often occupy the gap left between the experience of the board and the challenges of management and governance in a highly regulated, highly accountable environment. Much energy and time appears to fall into this domain of the principal's work. LDS articulates the challenge:

> It is clear that the conceptualisation of school leadership needs to be undertaken at system level, so that a clear articulation of a shared understanding of school leadership in education forms the basis for policy making and implementation in the field. (2007: 63)

The clear danger in the current practice is that the model of leadership currently operating in Ireland simply reinforces the compliant, managerial role of the 1970s and 1980s. This is not a criticism of managerialism per se; rather, I contend, that it creates an unwanted barrier to the full realisation of the potential of the principal's role as a leader of learning and of the school community. It is difficult to see how there can be any clear direction to the role of school leaders today until there is national consensus on the purpose of leadership, the skills, qualities, behaviours and practices of those who lead. This understanding can then inform who is selected for leadership positions and how they are supported and developed. Such an understanding could also aid in developing better understandings of the challenges facing all leaders in the school community, including Boards of Management members and the many teacher leaders who operate in positional roles such as formal middle management positions and informal leadership roles through authentic positive influence on school activity. Such an understanding is also necessary if there is to be a move from the more administrative-focused aspects of the role to a learning-centred approach as advocated by Byrne (2009) above.

Leadership practices

The Education Act 1998, Sections 22 and 23, refers to the leadership role of the principal teacher, both in terms of their managerial responsibilities and a broader aspiration for principal teachers to lead learning and teaching in schools. A range of measures including the development of middle management structures, the introduction of school development planning, a focus on whole-school evaluation and a general emergence of a culture of collaboration have contributed somewhat to the familiarisation of the isolation of the leadership role of the principal. For over a decade the formal middle management structures have supported school leaders, notwithstanding current embargoes on promotion. However, the model of leadership in most Irish schools remains largely hierarchical and atomised, with a focus on the distribution of tasks rather than responsibility. Elmore (2006) sees the improvement of practice as a collective endeavour with leadership being seen as more focused on the improvement and less on the role of the individual. The distributed leadership literature focuses on this need for communities of leaders and for a real distribution of power and responsibility as well as tasks. Leadership in such circumstances is no longer the privilege of the principal but a duty of all. Real distribution of leadership asks all to change, learn and build capacity to meet the needs of the school (Spillane et al., 2005; Elmore, 2006).

Just as in any attempt to refocus the purpose of leadership, it appears equally important that the invitation to lead be extended generously to those with the skills, commitment and ability to contribute to learning-centred leadership. Such aspirations are set against an Irish tradition of defining formal middle management roles quite narrowly and the genuine ambition of teachers to focus on classroom practice as opposed to management and leadership activity. A largely undocumented challenge for serving principals in particular is the extent to which others are invited to lead. O'Connor (2008) presents a troubled account of the

experiences of middle leaders in post-primary schools. This is characterised by leaders who feel unclear as to the nature of their responsibilities,
feel unsupported in their endeavours, and who are at times disillu-
sioned with the role they occupy. Central to their concerns is the relationship and support between them and the principal teacher. Hogan
et al. (2007) further subscribe to the claim that school principals have
considerable leverage over the ability of teachers to participate in
reform and improve practice in the wider school context.

Sergiovanni (2001) once compared leadership to getting an amoeba
to cross a road. The development of a community of leaders in Irish
schools over the past decade echoes this concept both in terms of the
remarkable progress and move towards collaboration that has taken
place and in terms of the considerable barriers to further unleashing
the distributed power of the collective. While having formal middle
leadership structures in place recognises the importance of a dispersal
of the leadership function and gives clarity to the organisation, the
distribution of leadership in the Irish educational context remains a
largely invitational process. It challenges school leaders to disperse
power and authority as well as functions. This does not lie easily with
the hierarchical construct of leadership, and it also challenges those
who represent school leaders to be more invitational in terms of the
national discourse around school leadership. The prevalence of
Ireland's rather heroic account of leadership activity is at variance
with Elmore's notion of the collective addressing the challenges of
improvement. Bennet et al. (2003) describe distributing school leadership as 'a way of thinking that challenges many current assumptions about leadership and the community in which it occurs'.

Leadership development

Over the past decade leadership development initiatives in Irish education have had considerable wind at their backs. The emergence of LDS
in 2002 was a statement of seminal intent on the part of the Department
of Education and Science and responded to a decade of proposals and
recommendations including OECD (1991), White Paper on Education
(Department of Education and Science, 1995) and Report of the
Working Group on the Role of the Primary School Principal (Department
of Education and Science, 1999). Since its inception LDS has initiated
a programme of leadership development that spans the career-long
learning advocated by OECD (2008, Vol. 1). All school principals now
receive a formal induction process and are given opportunities for
development later in their career. Leadership development has been
strengthened with support in school development planning and in

other school-based support programmes. Simultaneously the work of the principals' associations and other stakeholders has afforded school leaders a new range of development opportunities. Leadership development can be neither an event nor a programme. Rather it is the continuous accumulation of skills, practices and knowledge based on experience, formal learning, networking and interaction with colleagues. The recommendations of the OECD report (2008, Vol. 1) link the need to set out a clear profile of the knowledge, skills, attributes and successful practices of school leaders with coherent, continuous learning opportunities for practitioners.

Yet leadership development in Ireland is perhaps at a new crossroads. At a time of relative national austerity, professional development becomes a low-hanging fruit for a cuts agenda. Questions are (and will be) raised about who is responsible for leadership development, how it can be most efficiently delivered and what methods of development have maximum impact. Leadership development, if seen as a support service to school principals and deputy principals, is a luxury that Ireland can scarcely afford in the current economic climate. Leadership development, if seen as a high-leverage activity that offers the potential for empowering schools to build capacity, lead improvement and transform student growth becomes a powerful strategic weapon in the wise use of resources. What is probably most at stake is not so much the case for leadership development, or indeed the continuation of supply of services; rather it is the continuation of leadership development that is characterised by career-long learning, and is coherently linked to national expectations of school leaders as espoused in the OECD report. This coherence implies that leadership development can be provided by a plethora of providers but that there should be consistency of message, continuity and progression from the perspective of the practitioner.

Where do leaders come from? Where do they go?

Perhaps the greatest concern around the quality of school leadership in Ireland is the dearth of interest in many principalship positions. Lack of systematic data on the number of candidates applying for leadership positions leaves one relying on the flow of anecdotal tales of the lack of interest among teachers in leadership positions. This is particularly apparent in the case of the 2,000-plus smaller primary schools where the principal teacher has teaching duties. McKinsey and Company (2007) and Collins (2001) clearly point to the need to choose the right people for key positions. In the absence of choice, this would appear to be a game of chance. The lack of interest in moving into principalship is unfortunately mirrored by the increasing flow of school leaders who retire well before the mandatory retirement age. In 2003, LDS provided a leadership development service to 135 new primary and post-primary school principals on the Misneach Programme. As this was the initial year of the programme participation rates may have been significantly lower than in subsequent years. However, in 2009 over 320 new principals applied for the same programme, reflecting the dramatic rise in the turnover of school leaders.

The absence of published research on the reluctance of teachers to apply for principalships limits the discourse on succession planning. What is clear is that most teachers who apply for and who are appointed principal teacher do so for intrinsic reasons (Begley et al., 1990; Morgan and Sugrue, 2005). One suspects a close link between the excessively managerial dimension of the principal's role and some frustration at the barriers that keep principals away from meaty professional activity that impacts more directly on the teaching and learning agenda in schools. Indeed, teaching remains a highly sought after position in Irish schools and again one suspects that teaching offers the individual the type of professional fulfilment that is not as strong in principalship. New principals in Irish schools are somewhat surprised at the volume of paperwork and the manner in which it can take over one's professional activity (Morgan and Sugrue, 2005), suggesting a link between work–life balance issues and the lack of interest in principalship; a link already proven in Australia by Lacey (2000).

Finally, the role of school principal has been portrayed in a significantly negative light in the media and public discourse over recent years. The tales of work–life balance issues, lack of support and questions over pay differentials tend to overshadow the professional fulfilment that many new leaders feel on taking up principalship (Morgan and Sugrue, 2005). It is easy to understand why a teacher might be somewhat reluctant to leave teaching to take up principalship, given the image of the role that is now dominant in the media and educational circles.

What is increasingly apparent is that, for whichever of the reasons alluded to above, or for other reasons, school principalship in Ireland is not as attractive a role as one would wish to see in a progressive, dynamic professional domain. McKinsey and Company (2007) highlight the need to attract the highest possible candidates into teaching. School leadership roles are consistently attracting few candidates. The need to take steps to rectify this situation is urgent work as it is difficult to see how steps to develop, support, strengthen, share and encourage leadership will come to fruition if the desired quality and quantity of candidates do not present with an interest in senior leadership positions. This is an issue for the state, for employers, patrons and for all those who seek to support leadership as an attractive, rewarding pathway of progression for teachers.

Conclusion

School leadership in Ireland is located in a rich, complex educational past where for long periods leadership was provided by church and state as opposed to empowering the principal teacher to initiate, monitor and evaluate change at school level. From this tradition have emerged a deep national respect for teaching (iReach, 2010) and recognition of the provision of quality education in Ireland. For long periods the curriculum and the methodologies employed in schools were fixed and changed at a slow pace. The maelstrom of the late 20th and early 21st centuries has necessitated change at a pace few could have imagined a generation ago. Change demands leadership and a focus on the improvement and transformation of practices. School leadership has emerged as a considerable force in realising a change agenda in Irish education. The need for systematic change that empowers and sustains this leadership is ongoing. Leadership requires focus; requires collective action by those who govern schools and those who work in schools; requires the development of the knowledge and skills that underpin school improvement; and, above all, requires that the best potential leaders are motivated to take up leadership roles. Any refocusing on a more learning-centred role for school leaders can be strengthened by these considerations, but will also challenge the orthodoxy of practices towards a school environment where leaders (principal and others) are comfortable with an increased focus on classroom practices.

References

Begley, P., Campbell Evans, G. and Browning, A. (1990) 'Influences on the Socialising Experiences of Aspiring School Principals'. Annual Meeting of the Canadian Society for Studies in Education.

Bennet, N., Wise, C., Woods, P. and Harvey, J. (2003) *Distributed Leadership*. Nottingham: NCSL.

Byrne, C. (2009) 'Director's Update', in *Le Chéile*, 3: 127–31.

Collins, J. (2001) *Good to Great*. Boulder, Colorado: HarperCollins.

Coolahan, J. (1981) *Irish Education, History and Structure*. Dublin: Institute of Public Administration.

Department of Education and Science (1995) *Charting Our Education Future: White Paper on Education*. Dublin.

Department of Education and Science (1999) Report of the Working Group on the Role of the Primary School Principal. Dublin: The Stationery Office.

Elmore, R.F. (2006) 'Leadership as the practice of improvement', in OECD, *Improving School Leadership*, Vol. 2. Paris: OECD.

Fullan, M. (2006) *Quality Leadership – Quality Learning*. Cork: Líonra-IPPN.

Government of Ireland (1998) Education Act. Dublin: The Stationery Office.

Government of Ireland (2004) Educational Welfare Act and the Education of Persons with Special Educational Needs Act. Dublin: The Stationery Office.

Hallinger, P. and Heck, R. (1998) 'Exploring the Principal's contribution to school effectiveness 1980–1995', *School Effectiveness and School Improvement*, 9(2): 157–91.

Hogan, P., Brosnan, A., de Rósiste, R., MacAlister, A., Malone, A., Quirke-Bolt, N. and Smith, G. (2007) *Learning Anew*, TL21. Maynooth.

Huber, S. (2004) *Preparing School Leaders for the 21st Century*. London: Taylor and Francis.

INTO (1991) *The Role of the Principal Teacher: A Review*. Dublin: INTO.

iReach (2010) *Evaluating Public Attitudes to the Teaching Profession*. Maynooth: Teaching Council.

Lacey, K.A. (2000) *Survey on Succession Planning*. Melbourne: Victorian Department of Education.

Leader, D. and Boldt, S. (1994) Principals and Principalship: A Study of Principals in Voluntary Secondary Schools, Dublin: Marino Institute of Education.

Leadership Development for Schools (2002) *School Leadership – A Profile*. Ennis: Clare Education Centre.

Leadership Development for Schools (2007) *Improving School Leadership*. Ennis: Clare Education Centre.

Leithwood, K., Day, C., Sammons, P., Harris. A. and Hopkins, D. (2006) *Seven Strong Claims about Successful School Leadership*. University of Nottingham: NCSL/Department for Education and Skills,

McKinsey and Company (2007) *How the World's Best Performing Schools Systems Come Out on Top*.

Moore, A., George, R. and Halpin, D. (2002) 'The developing role of the headteacher in English schools, management, leadership and pragmatism', *Educational Management and Administration*, 30(2). London: Sage Publications.

Morgan, M. and Sugrue, C. (2005) *Evaluation of the Misneach Programme*. Ennis: Clare Education Centre.

NCSL (2006) *Learning-centred Leadership*. Nottingham: NCSL.

O'Connor, E. (2008) 'There is a lot to be learned: Assistant Principals' perceptions of their professional learning experiences and learning needs in their role as middle leaders in Irish PP schools'. Unpublished EdD thesis. Institute of Education, University of London.

OECD (1991) *Reviews of National Policies of Education – Ireland*. Paris: OECD.

OECD (2008) *Improving School Leadership, Vol. 1, Policy and Practice*. Paris: OECD.

OECD (2008) *Improving School Leadership, Vol. 2, Case Studies on System Leadership*. Paris: OECD.

Sachs, J. (2001) 'Teacher professional identity; competing discourses, competing outcomes', *Journal of Education Policy*, 16(2): 149–61.

Sergiovanni, T.J. (2001) *Leadership: What's In It For Schools?* London: Routledge Falmer.

Spillane, J.P., Diamond, J.B. and Franz Coldren, A. (2005) 'Distributing leadership', in M. Coles and G. Southworth (eds), *Developing Leaders; Creating the Schools of Tomorrow*. Berkshire: University Press.

Sugrue, Ciarán (2003) 'Principals' professional development: Realities, perspectives and possibilities', *Oideas*, 50.

Chapter 5

Autonomy and Accountability

Ciaran Sugrue

Abstract

Neo-liberal ideology has dominated international discourses of reform during the past two decades or more. Rhetorics of autonomy and the devolution of decision-making and responsibility to the level of the school have been accompanied by a recentralising discourse of greater curricular prescription and technologies of accountability. Yet these dominant discourses have been refracted differently within national policy arena due to different systemic traditions and trajectories. In the Irish context, as in other jurisdictions, self-evaluation has been promulgated as an antidote to creeping performativity. However, when Whole School Evaluation reports are critically analysed, there is little evidence of self-evaluation being recognised or promoted. Nevertheless, the language of accountability emerges as fluid and more open than elsewhere, thus presenting an important moment for school leaders and teachers to reshape the discourse, to re-inscribe professionalism, to move beyond technologies of control to a climate and culture of professional responsibility.

Key words

Autonomy; accountability; self-evaluation; performativity; leadership.

Introduction

In the context of 'liquid modernity' (see Bauman, 2000/2006) and the uncertainties and insecurities that are some of its hallmarks, school principals are expected to provide some situated certainty amidst competing agenda – a rhetoric of 'autonomy' and the constraining realities of regimes of internal and external accountability. Gross Stein captures something of the zeitgeist of this postmodern condition when she says, 'the paramount sin is now inefficiency. Dishonesty, unfairness, and injustice – the sins of the past – pale in comparison with the cardinal transgression of inefficiency' (Stein, 2001: 2).

Schools are a microcosm of larger social forces, part of international 'social movements'(Castells, 2000; Castells, 2004). School principals as leaders within school communities are pivotal actors in this 'drama' (Starratt, 1993), caught in the cross-wires of a competing if not conflicting policy agenda – empowered by 'autonomy' (Coghlan and Desurmont, 2007) whereby responsibility and decision-making have been devolved to the level of the school (Ireland, 1995); constrained and corralled by imposed regimes of accountability (Fink and Brayman, 2006; Hartle and Thomas, 2004; MacBeath et al., 2009). Despite a general tendency towards policy homogenisation internationally, such social movements or policy borrowing are 'refracted' (Goodson, 2004) differently within national borders due to different systemic traditions and trajectories (Sugrue, 2004).

The chapter is in four parts. Part one develops a multifocal theoretical lens by succinctly connecting rhetorics on autonomy, accountability and leadership from a variety of policy and research sources. Using this as a general backdrop it provides a more focused analysis of national accountability policy. Part two provides a brief account of the methods used for both the selection and analysis of data for the chapter. Part three, interrogates selected evidence regarding the manner in which primary principals are currently held to account, the extent to which self-evaluation contributes to the accountability agenda and shapes their leadership practices. Part four reflects on the evolution of this policy and practice, and in a more speculative manner suggests possible futures depending on power plays within the system.

Theoretical and policy considerations: autonomy, accountability & leadership

While it is generally accepted that a very dominant policy rhetoric has been 'autonomy', its history is far from homogeneous. Rather,'it is not a European tradition' and it is 'only since the 1980s that the movement towards school autonomy began to develop' (Coghlan and Desurmont, 2007, pp. 9–10). What such Brussels reports avoid is a language that would indicate the origins of these winds of change – a neo-liberal breeze that blew into a 'perfect storm'. At the very time that the private sector and financial services in general, were enjoying rather relaxed rules and regulations governing the manner in which they conducted their affairs, regimes of accountability were being imposed on systems of schooling. The confluence of these forces is 'all-pervasive within contemporary educational systems' and this is evident in the 'emphasis on policy as numbers' (Rose, 1999) and outcome accountability as empirical measures' (Lingard et al. 2003, p. 13). Nevertheless, the rhetoric seemed to continue to aspire to more noble ends – to ensure that 'every child matters' (DES, 2003; DES, 2004) and 'no child [would be] left behind' (NCLB, 2002). In general therefore, a top-down approach to the promotion of 'autonomy' as a policy position was imposed from the centre.

Re-regulation through regimes of external accountability led to the emergence of 'performativity' as a technology of control, with the following characteristics:

> ... not in any simple sense a technology of oppression, it is also one of satisfaction and rewards, at least for some. Indeed it works best when we come to want for ourselves what is wanted from us, when our moral sense of ourselves and our desires are aligned with the pleasures of performativity. But there is always the possibility of slippage between pleasure and tyranny within performativity regimes. (Ball, 2008: 52)

When accountability morphs into performativity, it may have both positive and negative consequences for leadership practice and pervades all aspects of school culture. As change accelerated to an unprecedented pace, the role of school principal was reshaped. Dimmock indicates something of this role diffusion when he states:

> However these terms [administration, management, leadership] are defined, school leaders experience difficulty in deciding the balance between higher order tasks designed to improve staff, student and school performance (leadership), routine maintenance of present operations (management) and lower order duties (administration). (Dimmock, 1996: 150)

Maintenance of the status quo was no longer regarded as adequate – 'transformational' leadership was now axiomatic (Leithwood et al.,

1996; Leithwood and Jantzi, 2000; Leithwood and Jantzi, 2005; Leithwood et al., 1999). As heroic forms of leadership were increasingly being questioned (Gronn, 1999; Gronn, 2003), and the complexity of the role made it impossible for any one individual no matter how 'super' (Copland, 2001; Reynolds, 2002), 'distributed' leadership (Spillane, 2006; Spillane and Diamond, 2007) became the latest in a proliferating 'adjectivalism' (Gronn, 2009) of leadership, with a tendency for policymakers to move well beyond what a more sober look at the empirical evidence actually suggests (Harris, 2008; Leithwood et al., 2009; Sugrue, 2009).

Internal and external accountability

Regimes of accountability, both internal and external are controversial and contested. However, it is generally accepted that 'self-evaluation and external evaluation reinforce the commitment of all of the key players, in and out of the school, to evaluate what they are doing' (MacBeath and McGlynn, 2002: 25) – internal and external as two sides of the same coin. In the Irish context, school inspection was seen as the prerogative of the inspectorate, thus it was largely something to be endured by teachers from time to time (see Sugrue, 1999).[1] Through a combination of policy borrowing and the influence of international agencies, there is a growing confluence of policy influences. In Scotland, England and Ireland, for example, the following policy documents arrived in sequence: *How Good Is Our School?* (HMIe, 1996), *School Evaluation Matters* (OFSTED, 1998) and *Looking At Our Schools: An Aid to Self-Evaluation in Primary Schools* (DES, 2003). However, when self-evaluation is promoted as being virtuous by those with responsibility for external accountability, there is considerable potential for sending mixed messages. In such circumstances, it becomes critical that teachers and schools have a very clear view of their responsibilities as professionals to 'speak for themselves' (MacBeath, 1999).

For internal and external accountability to function in complementary ways an appropriate synergy is required between: goals, their ongoing monitoring, well-documented evidence regarding specified goals and criteria, and transparency regarding an adequate audit trail while making this evidence available for appropriate scrutiny (Rudd and Davies, 2000; MacBeath and McGlynn, 2002).

National policies have been influenced in significant ways by a general move towards more tightly scripted regimes of control internationally (Sugrue, 2006). Suffice to say that the OECD report in 1991 was something of a catalyst (OECD, 1991), while the sequence of publications provided in the ensuing decade is an important 'audit trail'

(Lincoln and Guba, 1985) of the manner in which subsequent national policy evolved (DES, 1996; DES, 2002; DES, 2005; DES, 2006a; DES, 2006b; DES, 2006c; DES, 2006d; DES, 2006e; DES, 2006f; Sugrue, 2008b). The evolution of these policy prescriptions was crystalised in the 1998 Education Act, and copper-fastened centrally through 'partnership' agreements, particularly in *Towards 2016* (Taoiseach, 2006).

The Education Act (1998, see Section 5), rather like the Education Act of 1988 in the UK, or the No Child Left Behind (2001) legislation in the US, is a major landmark in the firmament of Irish education. The role of Section 5 is clear – to hold principals and teachers to account – while the manner in which these responsibilities are specified leaves one wondering about the relationship between self-evaluation as an internal professional responsibility and the external account compiled from snapshot visits by inspectors to the school.

Self-evaluation, external evaluation: spot the difference!

The basic structure of internal and external accountability was articulated more than a decade ago at a consultative conference on what was then called 'Whole School Inspection' (DES, 1996). This policy subsequently evolved through various iterations, but has largely remained focused on:

- the quality of school management;
- the quality of school planning;
- the quality of teaching and learning. (DES, 1996: 27)

This agenda was reiterated subsequently in *Looking at our School: An Aid to Self-evaluation in Primary Schools* (DES, 2003), followed by the *Guide to Whole School Evaluation* (DES, 2006c). Other systemic developments had a catalytic effect. After the Revised Primary Curriculum was published (Ireland, 1999), as part of the implementation strategy, two important support services were created – the Primary Curriculum Support Programme (PCSP) and the School Development Planning Service (SDPS).[2] Both services were answerable to the Inspectorate. There is a sense therefore in which SDPS in particular became the Trojan horse of the system, promoting self-evaluation, policy devised at the centre to be imposed on principals and teachers but mediated to principals and teachers by seconded colleagues. Apart from making the addition of 'support for students' there is little that distinguishes internal from external evaluation as indicated in Table 5.1.

These policy declarations clearly indicate a convenient seamless confluence of the internal self-evaluation as an aid to external evaluation,

Table 5.1   Self-evaluation and whole-school evaluation (WSE)

Themes for school self-evaluation at primary level	The evaluation framework
• Quality of school management • Quality of school planning • Quality of curriculum provision • Quality of learning and teaching in curriculum areas • Quality of support for pupils (DES, 2003: iii)	The WSE team evaluates and reports on the operation of the school under the following headings or areas of inquiry: • The quality of school management • The quality of school planning • The quality of learning and teaching • The quality of support for pupils (DES, 2006c, Section 3.2: 10)

an agenda underpinned by the Education Act 1998. The extent to which the 'reality' of these evolving policy perspectives is currently manifest in published reports is the focus of the empirical section of the chapter. First, a note on method is provided.

Method

Eleven WSE reports have been selected from those available for the first three years for which WSE reports have been published.[3] This selection partly reflects my ongoing interest in school leadership and in the most challenging contexts. Consequently, I sought to isolate large schools that are vertical (covering the entire age range four to 12), co-educational, and that at the time of inspection were designated disadvantaged. This purposive sample allows for a certain concentration, while seeking to make explicit the nature of accountability with particular reference to principals. As a consequence of these criteria being privileged as part of the process of sampling, analysis is confined to large urban schools in challenging circumstances. My initial intention was to include vertical schools only, but due to difficulties of identification, any school designated disadvantaged, whether junior, senior or vertical, was included, while the gender of the principal was accepted in the circumstances though initially a balance of gender was preferred. Although reports follow a standard format, each containing six sections, allowing for both variation and subsections or categories, data were coded into 27 open nodes using NVivo. In addition to the four 'themes' identified in Table 5.1, there is an introduction section, and section six provides 'summary of findings and summary of recommendations for further development'. Reports vary considerably in length, from approximately 5,500 words for the shortest, to more than twice that figure (11,700) in the case of the longest, but length may be a very poor yardstick of quality. The selective analysis that follows focuses initially on general observations, in-school management, self-evaluation, and recommendations, with a particular focus on the presence or absence of self-evaluation and its consequent impact on leaders and leadership.

WSE reports: general observations

The actual inspection process includes a pre-inspection meeting with the entire staff, a team of inspectors involved in the evaluation process depending on the size of the school, a post-inspection meeting at which a draft of the final report is presented orally, while the process also involves meetings with Board of Management members and parents. There is considerable variation in terms of the issuing of the final reports – from three to 12 months, with the more typical time lapse being six to seven months. The fact that only three Boards of Management availed of the opportunity to have their comments included in the final version may suggest a detachment from the process, but this warrants further investigation.

Making comparison between reports is rendered almost impossible due to lack of systematic use of terminology. Current practice seems more like a reversion to, or retention of, more idiosyncratic and bureaucratic approaches that characterised earlier reports and their content (Sugrue, 1999). In earlier documentation (DES, 1996) when performance indicators and performance criteria were indicated, a four-point scale was suggested: very good, good, fair and weak (DES, 1996: 2), but in practice this appears to be ignored. This is inconsistent with stated policy (DES, 2002; DES, 2006f)). Reports in general rely overwhelmingly on narrative accounts, and while this has attractions for a lay audience in terms of readability and accessibility, it does not preclude a much more standardised approach to the presentation of factual information. A report completed on a piloting of WSE identified one of the 'lessons' as being 'the need for quantitative information' (DES, 1999: 38).

Attempting to establish staff complements, for example, is extremely difficult, particularly with an increasing diversity of language support, learning resources as well as Special Needs Assistants, while none of the reports mention the presence of secretaries or caretakers, for example. A much more factual presentation of such evidence should be easily accomplished.

'In-school management'

The majority of reports provide a separate paragraph on the principal and then turn attention to the manner in which members of the middle management team discharge their responsibilities. However, there is often, for understandable reasons, a significant intertwining of the two. Nevertheless, there appears to be a hierarchy in which the work of members of middle management is described variously as: 'supporting the principal very effectively', 'supportive of the principal' and 'provides support for the principal'. While this is to be expected, the language used suggests delegation of responsibilities rather than a more collaborative shared or 'distributed' sense of the leadership enterprise (Spillane, 2006; Spillane and Diamond, 2007; Harris, 2008).

Principals – discharging their responsibilities?

Though these are 'schools on the edge' (MacBeath et al., 2007), the language in which this section of the reports is written is remarkably positive in tone and content. Although the details are difficult to decipher, eight of the 11 principals are female, some long-serving in that particular school, while in some instances they had considerable experience in that school prior to taking over the role of principal. There is need for much more systematic documentation of principal profiles to gain a more sophisticated understanding of leadership needs, particularly in a climate where increasingly there needs to be greater awareness than heretofore of fostering leadership potential within the teaching profession rather than leaving it to happenstance.[4] The language in this section is refreshingly positive and supportive, and much of the time also devoid of the language of new public management, in sharp contrast with the language of policy documents. Table 5.2 attempts to capture this by providing a key extract from each of the 11 reports.

Perhaps a systematic trawl of a much larger number of reports would reveal if this language is ubiquitous – devoid of a 'policy by numbers' mindset. It would be much more likely to indicate whether or not the inspectorate is in the process of generating a new language of evaluation in English, complete with the subtle gradations that were its forte when reports were written (almost exclusively) in Irish, and only insiders knew how to decipher them, and access was extremely restricted. A significant element of that graduated subtle language was often what was left unsaid, thus deciphering reports was also about reading between the lines. Meantime, some variation is detectable – a sort of 'summa cum laude', and a more ordinary laude or, as a divisional inspector once described to me, 'to damn with faint praise'.

Table 5.2 Holding principals to account

Principals: Key comments on their leadership (all quotes from reports)	
1 … clear sighted and dynamic	7 Visionary leadership
2 Highly effective	8 Visible leadership
3 Dedicated to the maintenance of high academic standards … friendliness … sense of purpose	9 Dedicated, conscientious and purposeful
4 Deeply committed and hardworking	10 Effective leadership characterised by dynamic enthusiasm and commitment. Displayed outstanding instructional leadership and creativity
5 She is very proactive in her leadership … committed and diligent manner	11 Enjoys the confidence and support of the teaching staff, board of management and parents …
6 She has given a lifetime of service to the education of the pupils at … as a dedicated and committed teacher initially and as principal for many years	

Middle management – shared leadership?

Middle management teams are described as supporting the principal. The language is similarly positive and upbeat, while the word used most frequently is 'support' or being supportive of the principal either 'very well' or 'very capably'. The following comment regarding relationships between principal and other team members is by no means exceptional: 'An excellent relationship exists between the in-school management team, principal and all staff members.' There was general commentary on the nature of responsibilities and the extent to which they complied with various circulars (07/03 and 17/00 in particular) whereby responsibilities assigned to members of the team should include curricular, organisational and pastoral duties. Where this was not happening or in long-established schools where posts were assigned on a more ad hoc basis, there was very clear recommendation captured most emphatically in the following: 'This report recommends that each curriculum area be assigned to a post holder so that the middle management team can further develop their individual roles as curriculum leaders for the school.' The general impression created is of a dedicated, motivated and committed workforce with a strong collaborative spirit and a sense of collective responsibility. Beyond the more general recommendation to have clarity regarding roles and responsibilities was the necessity to meet on a formal basis at regular intervals if this was not occurring already, and to report to boards of management regarding progress etc. There is a degree of old and new language being used in this context that sends mixed messages. There are individual responsibilities – thus a perpetuation of the old language of posts of responsibility, while each post holder is a member of a team – where flexibility, collaboration, shared responsibilities, along with collective leadership responsibility are part of the policy rhetoric as well as research literature. Arguably, greater formality and regularity regarding meetings and the necessity to record minutes and decisions, and to convey this to Boards of Management (BoMs) may be understood as a melange of self-evaluation while conscious also of legislative require-ments regarding accountability.

Self-evaluation

Self-evaluation, as the flip side of the external accountability coin, is an important means of protecting professional autonomy and exer-cising professional judgment. Since self-evaluation as a policy has been dictated centrally by the inspectorate, what evidence is there in WSE reports that it is perceived as an important element of the coin of the realm in an overall assessment of principals' and teachers' pro-fessional responsibility? An electronic word search for 'self-evaluation' in all 11 reports resulted in the term being found a total of four times only, two each in two reports, and in one of these the second was in a recommendation, directly referring to the first mention.

Significantly, in my view, comments regarding the importance of self-evaluation are made with reference to planning for inclusion of special needs learners in mainstream classrooms and the teachers are lauded for their efforts. The report states:

> The valid and purposeful nature of the planning process results in the formulation of policies and curriculum plans that reflect prac-tice in the classrooms that are relevant to the pupils in the school. They are meaningful and specific, which is congruent with the school's own self-evaluation and review of its plans. (Report extract)

The second mention of self-evaluation is in similar vein and refers to the manner in which good relations are fostered through the Home, School Community Liaison (HSCL) programme while being self-reflective about use of the term, referring to the quote above. It states: 'The relationship between school and home is defined by the open door policy articulated in the school's policy statements and self-evaluation as previously mentioned.' The only other occurrence of the term points to the absence of a standardised template for the recording of monthly progress, something that is now commonplace in many schools. While there is a compliance dimension to this comment, it does point to the potential of such a tool of accountability to enable staff to reflect on continuity and development of curricula throughout the school when it states: 'This resource could be used by staff to engage further in school self-evaluation, whereby work covered could be reviewed on a whole-school basis.'

In contrast with the minimal inclusion of self-evaluation in reports, the word planning is much more prominent. Notwithstanding the fact that the various headings and subheadings in the report template include the word planning approximately six times, there is one report only in which the word planning recurs more than 20 times, while in eight of the 11, the word occurs more than 30 times, with the highest number reaching 44. While a more in-depth interrogation of elements of reports dealing with planning is beyond the scope of the present analysis, on the basis of evidence presented here the value attached to professional self-evaluation as opposed to compliance with the production of the myriad of policy documents now a legal requirement seems to suggest a considerable imbalance. One means of attempting to shed additional light on this crucially important issue is to focus on the recommendations in these reports.

Recommendations

Recommendations are written in a concise 'bullet' point form. The smallest number is three, the maximum in one case is seven, four have four, two have five and one has six. There is a preponderance of emphasis on planning, the need for boards to develop policies regarding attendance, length of the school day, to review policies and to indicate dates for when they were reviewed, or the need to review SEN provision, Irish, Art, Pastoral Care. There is a strong emphasis on uniformity through the adoption of templates for short-term planning, and monthly progress records. However, six of the reports recommend greater attention to assessment for learning and further attention to record-keeping that facilitates more sophisticated use of assessment for teaching. There are recommendations for emphasis on more active learning pedagogies, that these be deployed with greater consistency and continuity throughout the school, and, in the process, to disseminate good practice, focus more on inclusion of SEN learners in mainstream classrooms, and plan for more differentiation within lessons. In some instances these requirements will necessitate making provision for peer classroom observation. While the majority of recommendations refer to policies and planning, the remainder deal with aspects of pedagogy of a general variety

Table 5.3 The language of recommendations

Needs more attention	Keep moving, extend in the right direction
'Priorities for action might be more clearly defined ...'	'extended as a strategy'
'... is advised to review and rationalise ...'	'should be developed ...'
'Merits attention'	'Continue to attend to ...'
'Needs to be reviewed'	'Continue to expand the practice'
'Avoid an over reliance on ...'	'... also be explored ...'
'... striking a better balance ...'	

while there are specific recommendations for individual schools re classroom resources for reading, place value, calculation, writing, as well as more general concerns regarding parental involvement and the use of assemblies. All of these may be construed as leadership concerns but they do not speak to leadership issues directly while the problem is how schools, without CPD budgets, are expected to bring about these changes under their own resources.

Recommendations that include phrases such as 'it is recommended that' (or an equivalent), 'as a priority' or 'should be developed immediately' leave little room for ambiguity. Beyond these 'directives' two categories of language urgency are detectable (see Table 5.3).

Conclusion

Analysis above indicates strongly the presence of the language of new public management, an integral element of the hegemonic influence of neo-liberal ideology, in a variety of policy documents. Yet, there appears to be a significant gap between the language of policy documents and the language of reporting. This lexical lacuna affords school leaders an enviable opportunity to influence the language of reporting and accountability, and to ensure that self-evaluation, as integral to the process of being professionally responsible, is reflected in WSE reports. There needs to be clearer articulation of the relationship between self-evaluation and external accountability, as neither current policy nor practice appears to have got to grips with this emerging agenda adequately, and, if self-evaluation does not seem to 'count' in WSE reports, the opportunity costs for principals and their colleagues may not be worth the investment. Middle management appears to be carrying a major portion of leadership responsibilities, but it may be necessary at this juncture to articulate more clearly understandings of a distributed perspective, while this in turn may have considerable implications for flexibility in staffing so that leadership capacity can be built within school communities in a systematic and sustainable manner. This needs to be accompanied by a more strategic approach to leadership capacity building at a school and system-wide level that embraces also a more elaborated understanding of the role of self-evaluation in fostering new forms of professionalism (Cunningham, 2008; Gewirtz et al., 2009).

Excessive demands for paperwork contribute to a climate of performativity, and the empirical evidence presented here tends to confirm such a view, though a more comprehensive analysis is also warranted. However, in terms of teachers in England and their experience of Ofsted, Irish primary teachers appear to have little to complain about (see Ofsted, 2008/09). Nevertheless, this is not an argument that seeks to deny the importance of responsibility, a term I prefer to accountability (see Sugrue and Dyrdal Solbrekke, forthcoming). Rather, for principals in particular, current economic and school realities present them with a major opportunity to assert the significance of self-evaluation as integral to their work and to act accordingly; to give leadership for learning the attention it deserves. Although self-evaluation may have been promoted as a central policy requirement, the extent to which performativity becomes more of a reality for principals and teachers in the immediate future will be determined largely by their capacity to forge new horizons of professional practice whereby self-evaluation becomes embedded in their emerging professional identities; the extent to which they domesticate this Trojan horse. Of course, appropriate professional support is also a systemic necessity. Facing up to this challenge is more likely to persuade the inspectorate to keep the language of reporting open, more flexible, less bureaucratic, notwithstanding the need for more systematic representation of school data. There is no guarantee that an appropriate balance between internal and external responsibilities may be forged, but without the leadership agency of the 'street level bureaucrats' (Lipsky, 1980) more performative dimensions of the role seem destined to dominate. Shaping the future is always a work in progress (Sugrue, 2008a). Self-evaluation may be the catalyst that catapults leaders beyond 'tinkering towards Utopia' (Tyack and Cuban, 1995) to genuine 'transformation' (West-Burnham, 2009).

Notes

1 It should be noted also that in the Irish context there are rather different traditions regarding school inspection at primary and secondary levels and these are frequently reflected also in teachers' attitudes towards external accountability—see (Coolahan with O'Donovan, 2009; Cunningham, 2009).

2 These separate and in some respects competing services were sensibly
   amalgamated in 2008.
3 This selection of reports for analysis had been undertaken at an earlier stage,
   thus it seemed sensible to work with data that had already been coded.
   Recent reading of more recently published reports suggest that in terms of
   structure and content they have not altered substantively.
4 In this regard, the Leadership Development for Schools (LDS) service has a
   critical role to play, and current economic realities will be a significant test of
   DES commitment to sustained support for building leadership capacity (for
   further information on this service see: http://lds21.ie).

References

Ball, S. (2008) 'Performativity, privatisation, professionals and the state', in
     B. Cunningham (ed.), *Exploring Professionalism* (pp. 50–72). London: Institute
     of Education.
Bauman, Z. (2000/2006) *Liquid Modernity*. Cambridge: Polity Press.
Castells, M. (2000) *The Information Age: Economy, Society and Culture Volume III:
     End of Millennium* (2nd edn, Vol. III). Oxford: Blackwell Publishing.
Castells, M. (2004) *The Information Age Economy, Society and Culture Volume II: The
     Power of Identity* (2nd edn). Oxford: Blackwell Publishing.
Coghlan, M. and Desurmont, A. (2007) *School Autonomy in Europe: Policies and
     Measures*. Brussels: Eurydice.
Coolahan, J. with O' Donnovan, P.F. (2009) *A History of Ireland's School Inspectorate
     1831–2008*. Dublin: Four Courts Press.
Copland, M.A. (2001) 'The Myth of the Superprincipal', *Phi Delta Kappan*, 82(7):
     528–33.
Cunningham, B. (ed.) (2008) *Exploring Professionalism*. London: Institute of
     Education.
Cunningham, J. (2009) *Unlikely Radicals: Irish Post-Primary Teachers and the ASTI,
     1909–2009*. Cork: Cork University Press.
DES (1996) *Whole School Inspection (WSI) Consultative Conference (13/03/96)
     Report*. Dublin: DES.
DES (1999) *Whole School Evaluation Report on the 1998/1999 Pilot Project*. Dublin: DES.
DES (2002) *Fifty School Reports: What Inspectors Say*. Dublin: DES.
DES (2003) *Looking At Our Schools: An Aid to Self-evaluation in Primary Schools*.
     Dublin: Government Publications.
DES (2005) *An Evaluation of Curriculum Implementation in Primary Schools: English,
     Mathematics and Visual Arts*. Dublin: Government Publications.
DES (2006a) *Cooperative School Evaluation Project (CSEP): A Study of the Development
     of Non-Curricular School Policies in a School Development Planning Context*.
     Dublin: Government Publications.
DES (2006b) *An Evaluation of Planning in Thirty Primary Schools*. Dublin: Government
     Publications.
DES (2006c) *A Guide to Whole School Evaluation In Primary Schools*. Dublin:
     Government Publications.
DES (2006d) *Publication of School Inspection Reports Guidelines*. Dublin: Government
     Publications.
DES (2006e) *Professional Code of Practice on Evaluation and Reporting for the
     Inspectorate*. Dublin: Government Publications.

DES (2006f) *A Guide to Whole School Evaluation in Post-Primary Schools*. Dublin: Government Publications.

Dimmock, C. (1996) 'Dilemmas for school leaders and administrators in restructuring', in K. Leithwood, J. Chapman, D. Corson, P. Hallinger and A. Hart (eds), *International Handbook of Educational Leadership and Administration* (Vol. 2, pp. 135–70). Dordrecht/Boston/London: Kluwer.

Every Child Matters (2003) Green Paper presented to Parliament by the Chief Secretary to the Treasury by Command of Her Majesty, September. London: HMSO.

Fink, D. and Brayman, C. (2006) 'School leadership succession and the challenges of change', *Educational Administration Quarterly*, 42(1): 62–9.

Gewirtz, S., Mahony, P., Hextall, I. and Cribb, A. (eds) (2009) *Changing Teacher Professionalism: International Trends, Challenges and Ways Forward*. New York and London: Routledge.

Goodson, I.F. (2004) 'Change processes and historical periods: an international perspective', in C. Sugrue (ed.), *Curriculum and Ideology: Irish Experiences, International Perspectives* (pp. 19–34). Dublin: The Liffey Press.

Gronn, P. (1999) *The Making of Educational Leaders*. London: Cassell.

Gronn, P. (2003) *The New Work of Educational Leaders: Changing Leadership Practice in an Era of School Reform*. London: Thousand Oaks and New Delhi: Paul Chapman Publishing.

Gronn, P. (2009) 'Hybrid Leadership', in K. Leithwood, B. Mascall and T. Strauss (eds), *Distributed Leadership According to the Evidence* (pp. 17–40). London and New York: Routledge.

Harris, A. (2008) *Distributed School Leadership: Developing Tomorrow's Leaders*. London and New York: Routledge.

Hartle, F. and Thomas, K. (2004) *Growing Tomorrow's School Leaders*. Nottingham: National College of School Leadership.

HMIe (1996) *How Good Is Our School: The Journey to Excellence*. Livingston: HMIe.

Ireland, Government of (1995) *Charting Our Education Future: White Paper on Education*. Dublin: Government Publications.

Ireland, Government of (1999) Primary School Curriculum Introduction. Dublin: Government Publications.

Leithwood, K., Chapman, J., Corson, D., Hallinger, P. and Hart, A. (eds) (1996) *International Handbook of Educational Leadership and Administration*. Dordrecht/Boston/London: Kluwer.

Leithwood, K. and Jantzi, D. (2000) 'The effects of transformational leadership on organisational conditions and student engagement', *Journal of Educational Administration*, 38(2): 112–29.

Leithwood, K. and Jantzi, D. (2005) *A Review of Transformational School Leadership Research*. Paper presented at the AERA.

Leithwood, K., Jantzi, D. and Steinbach, R. (1999) *Changing Leadership for Changing Times*. Buckingham: Open University Press.

Leithwood, K., Mascall, B. and Strauss, T. (eds) (2009) *Distributed Leadership According to the Evidence*. London and New York: Routledge.

Lincoln, Y. and Guba, E. (1985) *Naturalistic Inquiry*. New York: Sage Publications.

Lingard, B., Hayes, D., Mills, M. and Christie, P. (2003) *Leading, Learning, Making Hope Practical In Schools*. Maidenhead and Philadelphia: Open University Press.

Lipsky, M. (1980) *Street-Level Bureaucracy: Dilemmas of The Individual In Public Service*. New York: Russell Sage Foundation.

MacBeath, J. (1999) *Schools Must Speak for Themselves: The Case of School Self-Evaluation*. London: Routledge.

MacBeath, J., Gray, J., Cullen, J., Frost, D., Steward, S. and Swaffield, S. (2007) *Schools On The Edge: Responding to Challenging Circumstances*. London: Paul Chapman Publishing.

MacBeath, J., Gronn, P., Opfer, D., Lowden, K., Forde, C., Cowie, M. et al. (2009) *The Recruitment and Retention of Headteachers in Scotland (Report to the Scottish Government)*. Edinburgh: The Scottish Government.

MacBeath, J. and McGlynn, A. (2002) *Self-Evaluation: What's in it for Schools?* London and New York: Routledge.

No Child Left Behind Act of 2001 (NCLB) (2002) United States Act of Congress (January 2002).

OECD (1991) *Reviews of National Education Policies for Education: Ireland*. Paris: OECD.

OFSTED (1998) *School Evaluation Matters*. London: HMSO.

OFSTED (2008/09) *The Annual Report of Her Majesty's Chief Inspector of Education, Children's Services and Skills 2008/09*. London: The Stationery Office.

Reynolds, C. (ed.) (2002) *Women and School Leadership: International Perspectives*. Albany: SUNY.

Rose, N. (1999) *Powers of Freedom: Reframing Political Thought*. Cambridge: Cambridge University Press.

Rudd, P. and Davies, D. (2000) *Evaluating School Self-Evaluation*. Paper presented at the British Educational Research Association Conference, available from www.leeds.ac.uk/educo/documents/0000I641.htm

Spillane, J. (2006) *Distributed Leadership*. San Francisco: Jossey Bass.

Spillane, J. and Diamond, J.B. (eds) (2007) *Distributed Leadership in Practice*. San Francisco: Jossey Bass.

Starratt, R.J. (1993) *The Drama of Leadership*. London: The Falmer Press.

Stein, J. (2001) *The Cult of Efficiency*. Toronto: Anansi Press.

Sugrue, C. (1999) 'Primary school principals' perspectives on school evaluation: implications for professional development', *The Irish Journal of Education*, 29 & 30: 54–76.

Sugrue, C. (ed.) (2004) *Curriculum and Ideology: Irish Experiences, International Perspectives*. Dublin: The Liffey Press.

Sugrue, C. (2006) 'A critical appraisal of the impact of international agencies on educational reforms and teachers' lives and work: The Case of Ireland?', *European Educational Research Journal*, 5(3 & 4): 181–195.

Sugrue, C. (2008a) 'The plate tectonics of educational change in Ireland: consequences for research quality, policy and practice?', In C. Sugrue (ed.), *The Future of Educational Change: International Perspectives* (pp. 35–47). London & New York: Routledge.

Sugrue, C. (ed.) (2008b) *The Future of Educational Change: International Perspectives*. London & New York: Routledge.

Sugrue, C. (2009) 'From heroes and heroines to hermaphrodites: emancipation or emasculation of school leaders and leadership?', *School Leadership and Management*, 29(4): 361–372.

Sugrue, C. and Dyrdal Solbrekke, T. (eds) (forthcoming) *Professional Responsibility: New Horizons of Praxis*. London & New York: Routledge.

Taoiseach, D.o.A. (2006) *Towards 2016 Ten-Year Framework Social Partnership Agreement 2006–2015*.

Tyack, D. and Cuban, L. (1995) *Tinkering Toward Utopia: A Century of Public School Reform*. Cambridge, Massachusetts: Harvard University Press.

West-Burnham, J. (2009) *Rethinking Educational Leadership: From Improvement to Transformation*. New York and London: Continuum Books.

Chapter 6

Leadership and the Curriculum – a Question of Trust

Tom Collins and Rose Dolan

The teacher who seeks to give his pupils a wider horizon in literature does so at his peril. He will no doubt benefit his pupils, but he will infallibly reduce his results fees. As an intermediate teacher said to me, Culture is all very well in its way, but if you don't stick to your programme your boys won't pass. Stick to your programme is the strange device on the banner of the Irish intermediate system; and the programme bulks so large that there is no room for education.

(P.H. Pearse, 1879–1916)

Abstract

The view of curriculum depends largely on the lens through which one looks at it. In this chapter we explore curriculum as it unfolds when approached from the lens of trust. We show that different curricular emphases pivot largely on a view of the learner as one who can either be entrusted towards self-directed learning or as one for whom learning arises only as a by-product of a teaching experience. It contrasts a view of the classroom as a zone where the teacher has agency in the design and development of the curriculum with one where an externally generated and externally assessed curriculum is delivered.

Key words

Leadership; curriculum; trust; development; externally generated; self-directed learning; view of learner; view of school; curricular dispositions; pedagogy.

Concepts of curriculum

The concept of curriculum is a contested one. At one level it is sometimes construed as the story which one generation chooses to tell to the new generation. This, however, may be to see curriculum as a somewhat static generational memoir. To the extent that the notion of story conjures images of singularity or hegemony, it depicts curriculum as primarily inert; as amenable to delivery and as more or less passively received by those to whom it is delivered. Trant (2007) refers to this as curriculum as content, that is, the transmission of knowledge.

Curriculum may also be seen as a dynamic interaction between generations around a story which is itself constructed in the process of that interaction. To see curriculum in this way therefore is to see it more as a medium through which a generation views its world from the particular and historically unique position in which that generation finds itself. This is to view curriculum less as a story to be transmitted than as a process of creation in which the student has a central interpretational role in the process, actively constructs a world view and develops an understanding of his or her position within that arena.

A more expansive view of curriculum would see it as comprehending the totality of the schooling experience – the formal syllabus; the 'hidden curriculum', the extra-curricular and the subtext of cultural and organisational norms which underpin the school.

Views of schooling

Each of these views of curriculum is predicated on a particular view of the purpose of schooling. If the purpose of the school is to transmit knowledge, then it measures itself on the efficiency with which it does so with reference to the academic attainment levels of its student body. This view of curriculum is to see the school as a relatively passive delivery agent of a state syllabus in which neither the teacher nor the students have any particular emotional, intellectual or cultural investment. Freire (1970) refers to this as the 'banking model of education', where knowledge is deposited with the student to be withdrawn in the examination. Within this model, he describes the role of the teacher and students as follows:

(a) The teacher teaches and the students are taught;

(b) The teacher knows everything and the students know nothing;

(c) The teacher thinks and the students are thought about;

(d) The teacher talks and the students listen – meekly;

(e) The teacher disciplines and the students are disciplined;

(f) The teacher chooses and enforces his or her choice, and the students comply;

(g) The teacher acts and the students have the illusion of acting through the action of the teacher;

(h) The teacher chooses the programme content, and the students (who were not consulted) adapt to it;

(i) The teacher confuses the authority of knowledge with his or her own professional authority, which he or she sets in opposition to the freedom of the students;

(j) The teacher is the subject of the learning process, while the pupils are mere objects.

Freire contrasts this approach with that of the 'humanistic revolutionary educator' who must help the students:

> ... to engage in critical thinking and the quest for mutual humanisation. His efforts must be imbued with a profound trust in people and their creative power. To achieve this they must be partners of the students in their relations with them. (Freire, 1970: 75)

Freire's view of partnering with students would effect a profound change in the teacher–student relationship, moving the teacher from a process of instruction to one of enabling a process of exploration and creation. A view of curriculum as a process of creation would see the school as committed to meeting the current developmental needs of the students, grounded in the conviction as expressed by Dewey that the best preparation for future life is a full life in the present. Dewey held that the purpose of formal education was not to prepare children for any fixed destination, but to enable children to grow and develop towards adulthood. He did not regard childhood as merely a prelude to adulthood but as a distinctive and unique developmental stage in its own right (Dewey, 1916).

Such a focus would encompass the intellectual development of the student together with his/her emotional, social, psychological and cultural development. Within this model the view of curriculum will be less prescriptive and more likely to emerge in the form of a curricular framework than in a tightly defined syllabus.

The third view of curriculum sees school as a microcosm of the larger society, where relationships, roles and achievements within the school will tend to replicate those of the wider society. This view of curriculum is well captured in Bourdieu's concept of habitus.

Bourdieu's description of habitus as a series of dispositions, a structure that is lived in, practised and enacted is described in his *Outline of a Theory of Practice* (1977). If the dispositions are the invisible component of the human, then the actions and practices of the individual are these dispositions made visible. As the practices produced by habitus become strategy-generating principles, they enable the person to 'cope with unforeseen and ever-changing situations' (1977: 72). Practices emerge from habitus, reproduce it and may occasionally challenge it. Therefore, once habitus is known, the behaviour becomes understandable. The corollary to this indicates that if the behaviour is interrogated, the structuring principles may be deduced and habitus becomes visible. As Bourdieu and Wacquant put it:

> When habitus encounters a social world of which it is the product, it finds itself 'as a fish in water', it does not feel the weight of the water and takes the world about itself for granted. (Bourdieu and Wacquant, 1992: 43)

This is to see school as a zone where the dominant social patterns are more or less reproduced on an intergenerational basis if not actively interrogated and challenged. The literature on the 'hidden curriculum' (Jackson, 1968) for instance draws attention to the values, norms and practices which underpin the structure and culture of the school but which are largely invisible in their normality.

Curricular dispositions in Ireland

It can be suggested that much curricular change, particularly in the area of pedagogical developments, is predicated on changing mutual expectations and perceptions between teachers and students. Much of this change in Ireland was pioneered in and is derived from the informal Adult and Community Education sector which was heavily influenced in the 1970s and 1980s by the work of Paolo Freire on the one hand and that of Carl Rogers on the other.

The Rogerian approach to counselling and therapy is underpinned by a fundamental reappraisal of the person's capacity for self-healing, self-awareness and self-actualisation. It is significant that Rogers began life as an agriculturalist where he is likely to have developed a keen awareness of the conditions for growth and an understanding of the power of an enabling nutritious environment in supporting growth as well as an awareness of the systemic nature of organic life. Given a propitious set of circumstances, he saw human growth as inevitable, as captured for instance in the following:

> ... individuals are able to trust their total organismic reaction to a new situation because they discover to an ever-increasing degree that if they are open to their experience, doing what 'feels right' proves to be a competent and trustworthy guide to behavior which is truly satisfying. ...The hypothetical person who is fully open to his experience would have access to all of the available data in the situation, on which to base his behavior; the social demands, his own complex and possibly conflicting needs; his memories of similar situations; his perception of the uniqueness of the situation. The data would be very complex indeed. But he could permit his total organism, his consciousness participating, to consider each stimulus, need and demand, its relative intensity and importance, and out of this complex weighing and balancing, discover that course of action which would come closest to satisfying all his needs in the situation. (Rogers, 1961: 189–90)

The Rogerian view of the person as innately capable and agentic would have a significant bearing on thinkers in the area of adult learning, particularly on the work of Malcolm Knowles and his concept of Andragogy. Knowles initially based andragogical theory on a number of assumptions that differed from those of pedagogy. These were:

- Self-concept: the assumption is that as a person matures his self-concept moves from one of being a dependent personality toward one of being a self-directed human being.
- Experience: the assumption that as a person matures he accumulates a growing reservoir of experience that becomes an increasing resource for learning.
- Readiness to learn: the assumption that as a person matures his readiness to learn becomes oriented increasingly to the developmental tasks of his social roles.
- Orientation to learning: the assumption that as a person matures his time perspective changes from one of postponed application

of knowledge to immediacy of application, and accordingly his orientation toward learning shifts from one of subject-centeredness to one of problem centeredness. (Knowles, 1973: 45–8)

- Motivation: the motivation to learn is internal rather than external. (Knowles et al., 1984: 12)

While Knowles clearly is of the view that adult learners can be entrusted with their own learning, his view that children learn differently from adults is a deeply problematic one, particularly when viewed through the work of thinkers in the area of early childhood learning, many of whom long predated Rogers and Knowles. In the 1840s, Friedrich Froebel (1782–1852) would develop the *kindergarten* movement drawing attention to the power of play in learning. A little later the work of Rudolf Steiner (1861–1925) would place children at the centre of their own learning, recognising the importance of the emotional and developmental stage of the child in meeting particular learning challenges. Maria Montessori (1870–1952), founder of the Montessori school movement, emphasised the power of children learning from each other and the centrality of an enriching environment in the learning process.

In late 20th-century Ireland, the work of many of these thinkers would have a major influence on the development of a vibrant adult and community education sector on the one hand and the growing early childhood and preschool sector on the other. Both of these sectors had a common character of being outside of the formal school system. It is noteworthy that official education policy in Ireland took little note of these sectors up until the end of the 1990s. The Education Green Paper of 1992 was silent on its philosophical assumptions and the White Paper of 1995 largely ignored both sectors and seemed unaware of many of the innovations that were then being pioneered in these settings. It was with the launch of the new primary curriculum in 1999 that the first major curricular transformations in the development of a child-centred and child-active curriculum in formal education began to gain expression. This approach allows for much greater creative engagement by teacher and student with the emphasis on child-centred learning.

There is a growing body of anecdotal evidence, however, that as the child proceeds through primary school, the child-centred emphasis begins to be dissipated as the focus of teacher attention shifts from the current developmental needs of the child to the future task of entering second level and meeting the academic demands of that environment. This prospect may also underpin the growing pressure to increase the subject load at primary level – on the assumption that the children will be better positioned to tackle these subjects at second level if they have already encountered them at primary. This move away from a child-centred curriculum is accentuated at second level, driven as it is by 'extrinsic goals' such as third level entry rather than by any goals which are particularly intrinsic by the developmental needs of the adolescent within the second level system.

Curricular challenges in the 21st century

In 1969, Peter Drucker published his seminal work, *The Age of Discontinuity*. In this work, Drucker identified four areas of profound discontinuity between the past and the future. These were new technology, mass media, globalisation and pluralism. There is a sense in which new technology is in fact the overarching discontinuity, as it has been the developments in Information and Communications Technology (ICT) which have made possible the emergence of a new economy based on information and which have enabled the globalisation of knowledge and markets and allowed for the emergence of a 'global shopping centre' in much the same way as that anticipated by Drucker 50 years ago. Drucker bemoaned the absence of global institutions capable of managing an unstable new world economy. The absence of such institutional capability has emerged in the early 21st century as a problem not only in managing the marketplace but even more so in managing and addressing the global environmental challenge – a challenge which incidentally Drucker failed to anticipate in 1969.

Drucker's theme of discontinuity is picked up by Marc Prensky (2001) in exploring the impact of new technology on education. He argues that today's 'students have changed radically … [they] are no longer the people our education system was designed to teach … a really big *discontinuity* [italics in original] has taken place. One might even call it a "singularity" – an event which changes things so fundamentally that there is no going back. This … is the arrival and rapid dissemination of digital technology of the last decades of the 20th century' (Prensky, 2001:1). Prensky goes on to refer to the generation of teachers who predate the digital revolution as 'Digital Immigrants' as opposed to the 'Digital Natives' born into the computer age and all 'native speakers of the digital language of computers, video games and the internet'.

Prensky's analysis is however only part of the picture captured by Drucker's concept of discontinuity. The challenge which new technology represents to education is a considerably wider one. Ever since Drucker's seminal work, there has been a growing international consensus on the place of knowledge as a key economic resource and of the role of education systems in supporting knowledge economies – if not necessarily knowledge societies. Working in a competitive global environment, individual countries are concerned to achieve competitive advantage in the knowledge domain and consider a well-functioning education system as critical to this process.

> With this new emphasis on learning we seem to be moving towards a 'learning economy' where the success of individuals, firms, regions and countries will reflect more than anything else their ability to learn. This raises profound questions as to the kind of knowledge that schools are imparting and ought to impart to their students. (OECD, 2001: 29)

The OECD view of the school as 'imparting knowledge' is of course predicated on a particular view of curriculum as referred to above and also on a particular view of the school as organisation.

When looked at from a socio-historical perspective, the school as organisation may be seen in four ways: school as custody, as factory, as service centre and as community. The different elements of each of these broad categories may be represented as shown in Table 6.1.

A view of the school as custody would draw on the work of Erving Goffman, particularly on his concept of total institutions (1961). He saw total institutions as those in which blocks of people are bureaucratically processed while being physically isolated from the normal round of activities, by being required to sleep, work and play within the confines of the same institution. While schools typically do not conform to the entirety of a total institution as

Table 6.1   The school as custody, factory, service centre and community

	Custody	Factory	Service centre	Community
Student is	inmate	raw material	customer	member
Outcome	rehabilitated	competitive	satisfied	contributor
Order	care and punishment	mechanistic	customer choice	organic
Role of teacher	custodian	delivers	serves	facilitates
Social project	compliant	useful	informed consumer	responsible
Learning project	behaviour modification	follow instructions	attain personal goals	co-learning

described by Goffman, there is much to his construct to which schools accord, most particularly the tendency towards the 'bureaucratic regimentation' of staff and students and the tendencies towards resistance within the 'underlife' – of the school culture.

A view of the school as factory draws upon the work of Toffler, particularly his 'wave theory' (1980). Here Toffler proposed a view of history as consisting of three waves: the agricultural, industrial and post-industrial. He saw the factory as the defining institution of the second wave, industrial era. This wave was underpinned by what Toffler referred to as a code which consisted of six universal principles. These were standardisation, synchronisation, concentration, specialisation, maximisation and centralisation. When applied to the school, these principles become apparent, for example, in the use of standard texts and tests; in complex synchronised timetables; in the concentration of particular age groups in designated year groupings; in the teaching of discrete subject areas by subject specialists; in the tendency towards the creation of larger classes and schools on grounds of efficiency and choice; and in the centralisation of decision-making, be it at local or at national levels.

A view of the school as service centre would look to Hargreaves' (2004) concept of a 21st century educational imaginary which he describes as follows:

- Students' identities and destinies are fluid;
- Intelligences are multiple, plastic and learnable;
- Schools are culturally heterogeneous;
- Schools are diverse;
- Education is lifelong, formal and informal;
- Education is unconstrained by time and place;
- Roles are blurred and overlapping;
- Schools and teachers are embedded in complex and interconnected networks;
- Education is user-led;
- Schools are designed for personalised learning.

Within this model of school, the student makes informed choices on a self-directed and self-interested basis, replicating all other relationships within the marketplace.

This view of school as service centre, however, ignores the possibilities of a more normatively driven schooling which would see the school as a counterforce to the wider dominant ideologies of the marketplace and as one which provides a 'safe haven' for children, allowing them an experience of being nurtured and of optimising their abilities. As with the earlier two models of school as custody and school as factory, the service centre view of school is a low-trust view, predicated on the capacity of the individual to compete in a self-interested and asocial context.

A view of school as community emphasises its normative role in society drawing attention to the 'moral development' of the child, in other words the child's sense of developing his or her responsibility to the group. As such, it is a somewhat subversive view of the over-riding concern with competitiveness, foregrounding values of and preoccupations with collaboration, cooperation and personal well-being. Insofar as it empowers the school to create appropriate locally generated responses to the developmental needs of its members, it is a high-trust view of the school, school leaders, teachers, the student body and the wider school community.

The changing nature of pedagogy and content

The debate and processes of organisational change in the 21st-century school are mirrored in the area of pedagogy and content. As mentioned earlier, the demands of a knowledge economy and a knowledge society have become very explicitly articulated in much of the contemporary thinking on curriculum. Much of this debate centres around the issue of 'core skills' or 'key skills'.

Historically, the move from a reliance on resources based on commodities to one based on knowledge is succinctly captured by Hogan in the following:

> ... following the transformations wrought by the Industrial Revolution, a particular importance was more widely given to natural resources such as coal, iron ore, copper, oil and mineral deposits. In a globalised era, often referred to as a 'post-industrial' age, a new category of resources has come to prominence, namely 'human resources'. Such resources at the more rudimentary level include a literate workforce capable of benefiting quickly from training and retraining. The ability to take initiatives and to work in teams is also becoming a sought-after quality in employees. At more advanced levels, highly valued human resources include: a supply of entrepreneurs and business leaders; a managerial corps that can efficiently monitor performance and either forestall or minimise industrial relations difficulties and a body of advanced researchers capable of furnishing innovations that have important commercial applications. (Hogan, 2010: 21–2)

Considerations such as those described by Hogan tend to underpin the case for investment in education on the one hand while also impacting on the specific organisational and syllabus content decisions within education on the other. Much of this latter debate, regarding curricular content, is concerned with an area that has come to be known as 21st century skills. The development of these skills is at the forefront of educational reforms in many countries – USA, Australia, New Zealand, Canada, Hong Kong, England and Ireland, to name but a few.

In Ireland in 2006, the National Council for Curriculum and Assessment (NCCA) set up a school network to implement five skills that have been 'identified as central to teaching and learning across the curriculum at senior cycle. These are information processing, being personally effective, communicating, critical and creative thinking and working with others' (NCCA, 2008: 5). The interim report on key skills at senior cycle described five key findings from the implementation of a key skills approach in the following subjects at senior cycle; Mathematics, Biology, English, French, Irish and Spanish. These findings are as follows:

1 The five key skills are relevant to each subject;
2 Teachers claim that when key skills are the focus in planning for teaching then teaching becomes more learner-centred;
3 For teachers to be successful in embedding the key skills, they needed to be given opportunities to develop their own understanding and practice of the key skills;
4 The successful embedding of key skills requires curriculum and assessment change;
5 Teachers and students claim that a key skills approach to teaching contributes to effective learning.

While each of the findings is significant in its own right, two clear messages emerge from this. One is that the opportunity for professional development of teachers in these key skills is essential for the development of the key skills with the students. This puts 'teacher retraining' as a central topic rather than the tacked on version described by Clandinin and Connelly as follows:

Generally speaking, learner, subject matter and milieu are well represented in the literature. But in most of the literature, the teacher as a focus for curriculum discourse tends to be minimized and treated in derivative ways. At the risk of oversimplifying, many milieu curriculum arguments tend to treat the teacher as an unconscious reproducer of inequitable social structures; many subject matter arguments demand rationalistic disciplinary training of teachers; and learner based arguments tend to see the teacher as nurturer. In almost all such curriculum proposals 'teacher retraining' is tacked on to the more central topic. (Clandinin and Connelly, 1990: 246)

Curricular change has generally been perceived as a change in subject content with little attention paid to the development of appropriate pedagogical strategies for the teachers who will implement the new curriculum. But such skills cannot be taught to teachers in an isolated fashion. Rather there is need for a different model of professional development of teachers that is situated in schools and in classrooms on an ongoing basis rather than at one-day seminars delivered in isolation from the specific school context. The model of professional development employed in the research project *Teaching and Learning in the 21st Century (TL21)* is one that would integrate with a key skills approach. In this study, an action research model was used to enable teachers to *become the authors of their own work* in developing at the classroom level new pedagogical approaches with the emphasis on active learning. As with other similar approaches, the TL21 project drew attention to the need for a less content-heavy syllabus but for more teacher autonomy in deciding both the content appropriate to the development of these skills and the pedagogical approach most appropriate to their development. (Further information about the TL21 project, including the interim and final reports, is available at http://www.nuim.ie/TL21/) The Finnish model, where the teacher is the primary curriculum planner, or indeed the English model, where a number of different curricula exist for the same subject, would appear more appropriate to a focus on key skills.

The second clear message from these findings is that not only the curriculum but also very particularly the mode of assessment needs to change. This is firstly to place a greater emphasis on formative assessment as opposed to summative assessment. It also requires a multiplicity of assessment approaches, moving away from the literary mode of assessment as the default position in assessment and also aiming to validate along the continuum of intelligences as described by Gardner (1983, 2006).

It is clear therefore that this change is a multifaceted one. It requires a different view of subject knowledge both from teachers, the subject experts, and from students, many of whom have absorbed a view that learning is the memorisation and reproduction of factual information. A change in this low-trust view of education and schooling requires a significant paradigmatic shift, not only on the part of the teacher and student, but also on the part of society.

These changes are likely to come about only with a profound overhaul of how the assessment of learning happens and in the context of a wider societal and political agreement that traditional assessment systems are no longer fit for purpose and can even be counterproductive in supporting the requirements of critical thinking, creativity and intellectual and social agility required of 21st-century learners.

This of course raises the question of who can be entrusted to lead these changes. The evidence is that this kind of change must be led from the classroom by teachers interacting with their students and with their subject in new ways and being enabled to provide assurance to the wider society of the quality and the value of their work. A pattern of teaching to the test is one where the demands of accountability subvert all principles of appropriate pedagogy, of child-centred learning and of the professional autonomy of the teacher. A leap of trust in these key actors in the educational system is the first requirement of policymakers if this change is to occur.

References

Bourdieu, P. (1977) *Outline of a Theory of Practice* (translated by Richard Nice). Cambridge: Cambridge University Press.

Bourdieu, P. (1990) *The Logic of Practice* (translated by Richard Nice). Cambridge: Cambridge University Press.

Bourdieu, P. and Wacquant, L. (1992) *An Invitation to Reflexive Sociology.* Chicago: The University of Chicago.

Clandinin, D.J. and Connelly, F.M. (1990) 'Narrative, experience and the study of curriculum', *Cambridge Journal of Education*, 20(3).

Dewey, J. (1916) *Democracy and Education.* New York: Macmillan.

Drucker, P.F. (1969) *The Age of Discontinuity; Guidelines to our Changing Society.* New York: Harper and Row.

Freire, P. (1970) *Pedagogy of the Oppressed.* New York: Herder and Herder.

Gardner, H. (1983) *Frames of Mind: The Theory of Multiple Intelligences.* New York: Basic Books.

Gardner, H. (2006) Five minds for the future. Boston: Harvard Business School Press.

Goffman, E. (1961) *Asylums: Essays on the Social Situation of Mental Patients and Other Inmates.* New York and Toronto: Anchor Books.

Hargreaves, D. (2004) *Personalising Learning: Next Steps in Working Laterally.* London: Specialist Schools Trust.

Hogan, P. (2010) *The New Significance of Learning: Imagination's Heartwork.* London and New York: Routledge.

Jackson, P. (1968) *Life in Classrooms*. New York : Holt, Rinehart and Winston.

Knowles, M. (1973) *The Adult Learner: A Neglected Species*. Texas: Gulf Publishing Company.

Knowles, M.S. et al. (1984) *Andragogy in Action. Applying Modern Principles of Adult Education*. San Francisco: Jossey Bass.

NCCA (2008) *Key Skills at Senior Cycle: Interim Report*. Dublin: NCCA.

OECD (2001) *Schooling for Tomorrow. What Schools for the Future*. Paris: OECD.

Pearse, P.H. (1879–1916) *The Murder Machine and Other Essays*. Dublin: Mercier Press.

Prensky, M. (2001) *'Digital Natives, Digital Immigrants'*, On the Horizon, 9(5). MCB University Press, downloaded from www.marcprensky.com/.../Prensky%20-%20 Digital%20Natives,%20Digital%20Immigrants%20-%20Part1.pdf 13 July 2010.

Rogers, C. R. (1961) *On Becoming a Person: A Therapist's View of Psychotherapy*. Boston: Houghton Mifflin.

Toffler, A. (1980) *The Third Wave*. London: Collins.

Trant, A. (2007) *Curriculum Matters in Ireland*. Dublin: Blackhall.

Chapter 7

Leadership and Teacher Education

Paul F. Conway, Rosaleen Murphy,
Kathy Hall and Anne Rath

There are no formal structures, arrangements or requirements in relation to teacher observation, coaching or mentoring ... While there is no tradition of teacher observation, peer coaching or mentoring in Ireland, there have been a number of pilot projects involving groups of schools and Education Centres in which different approaches to mentoring have been monitored and researched.

(OECD/LDS, 2007: 43–4)

Nowhere is the absence of a seamless continuum in teacher education more evident than in the early years of teaching. At the same time, no point in the continuum has more potential to bring the worlds of the school and the academy into a true symbiotic partnership than the induction phase.

(Howey and Zimpher, 1999: 297)

Abstract

The central argument in this paper is that deeper engagement with pedagogy must be a hallmark of teacher education in order to promote curriculum reform, enhance teacher professionalism and nurture leadership in the coming years. First, we situate understandings of good or quality teaching in a socio-political context. Second, we comment on the context of schooling in Ireland. Third, we address the issues of school culture supportive of ITE and induction as well as the challenge of promoting deep engagement with pedagogy. In particular, we focus on the implications for teacher education of one of the findings of the recent OECD's TALIS report (Gilleece et al., 2009): that professional collaboration in schools is characterised by a focus on exchange and sharing rather than on deeper levels of professional engagement centred on classroom pedagogy as noted above. Finally, guided by the principle of deepening engagement on pedagogy, we identify four key priorities for leaders in advancing research, policy and practice in teacher education: (i) observation in peer classrooms, (ii) sharing and talking about practice, (iii) representing practices through profiles and portfolios, and (iv) models of school–university partnership.

Key words

Teacher learning; professional collaboration; 'horizon of observation'; pedagogy; teacher education; profession; curriculum reform.

Introduction: the observability of teaching

Two studies almost 20 years apart provide food for thought in relation to the nature of teachers' professional learning in Irish schools and its implications for teacher education. In 1991 the OECD country review of Ireland's education system noted what the review team termed the 'legendary autonomy' of Irish teachers. In 2009, the OECD's *Teaching and Learning International Survey* (TALIS) (Gilleece et al., 2009) identified a distinct pattern of teacher collaboration across participating countries – including Ireland. That is, the dominant form of professional collaboration is characterised by what the study termed 'exchange and coordination' activities more frequently than 'more complex professional collaboration', the latter involving activities such as jointly teaching the same class, taking part in year or subject area meetings, observing another teacher's class and providing feedback, engaging in joint activities across different classes and age groups (for example, projects) and discussing and coordinating homework practice across subjects (Gilleece et al., 2009: 84). Furthermore, the OECD/LDS report on leadership in Irish schools noted that 'There are no formal structures, arrangements or requirements in relation to teacher observation, coaching or mentoring' (2007: 43). Cogniscent of these observations, this chapter focuses on the nature of professional collaboration in the context of initial teacher education. When pedagogical solitude characterises the practice of teaching, and exchange and coordination level activities typify teachers' collegial relations, there are inadequate opportunities collectively to see, understand and develop pedagogy. Consequently, with the heart of schooling remaining largely unobservable by peers, opportunities for professional learning are significantly foreclosed – with, we argue, significant implications for initial teacher education and induction.

It is in this context that the chapter explores what new understandings of quality teacher education, which elevate the importance of deep engagement with pedagogy at the initial and induction phases of the continuum, might mean for teacher education leadership in schools and higher education institutions in Ireland. Teacher education is challenged by both societal change and educational change. These challenges form the work context for the recently established Teaching Council in Ireland.

Adopting a sociocultural perspective (Hall et al. 2008), we focus on the opportunities to learn to teach in initial teacher education (ITE), drawing on findings from a Teaching Council-commissioned recent nine-country study (Conway et al., 2009). Our focus on deepening engagement with pedagogy is informed by the sociocultural concept 'horizon of observation,' that is:

> Lines of observation and limits on observation of the activities of others have consequences for the knowledge acquisition process ... Let us refer to the outer boundary of the portion of the task that can be seen or heard by each team member as that person's horizon of observation. (Hutchins, 1993: 52)

In doing so we argue that the horizon of observation available to students in ITE and newly qualified teachers (NQTs) on induction is limited by current structural and cultural arrangements – notwithstanding the existing significant support available to ITE students and NQTs in schools. For example, the Department of Education and Skills-funded UCC *Learning to Teach Study* (LETS) of the Postgraduate Diploma in Education (PGDE) found that 'In the case of the PGDE students, their "horizon of observation" is significantly limited, despite the widespread access to one or more types of mentors. Even for the 40% who did have observation opportunities, these were rare events, with one in six experiencing this once or twice, and a similar number having opportunities to talk to the observed teacher following the lesson' (Conway et al., 2010a: 111). As such, the strong cultural dynamic of autonomous teaching and professional collaboration focused mainly on coordination issues seems to have a significant impact on student teachers' horizon of observation (Conway, 2010).

This chapter is divided into four sections. First, we situate under-standings of good or quality teaching in a socio-political context. Second, we comment on the context of schooling in Ireland. Third, we address the issues of school culture supportive of ITE and induc-tion as well as the challenge of promoting deep engagement with pedagogy. In particular, we focus on the implications for teacher edu-cation of one of the findings of the recent OECD's TALIS report (Gilleece et al., 2009): that professional collaboration in schools is characterised by a focus on exchange and sharing rather than on deeper levels of professional engagement centred on classroom peda-gogy as noted above. Finally, guided by the principle of deepening engagement on pedagogy, we identify four key priorities for leaders in advancing research, policy and practice in teacher education: (i) observation in peer classrooms, (ii) sharing and talking about prac-tice, (iii) representing practices through profiles and portfolios, and (iv) models of school–university partnership.

Understanding good teaching: socio-political dynamics

Heightened expectations of teachers have led to an unprecedented political, professional and research interest in the theory and practice of teacher education worldwide. This is evident in the number of reviews in various countries and cross-national studies of teaching and teacher education in the past few years, including OECD's *Teachers Matter* (2005), McKinsey Report *How the World's Best Performing School Systems Come Out on Top* (Barber and Mourshed, 2007), World Bank's *Learning to Teach in the Knowledge Society* (Moreno, 2005) and UNESCO's *Education for All: The Quality Imperative* (2005). In their different ways all these reports highlight the fact that the 'quality imperative' requires a fresh look at various aspects of teacher education. All of them high-light the need for a new extended teacher professionalism characterised by greater collegiality than was typical in the past, by a recognition of the increasing complexity of professional practice, by awareness of the challenges of teaching a more diverse student body to higher levels of academic attainment, and of the challenges posed by the imperatives of equality and inclusion. Furthermore, the contemporary policy inter-est in teacher education is based on an assumption that 'the formula-tion of policy and the design of teacher preparation and continuing professional development optimally takes into account the whole spectrum of teacher learning, that is, teachers' opportunities to learn from their own prior schooling and throughout their own teaching careers' (Schwille and Dembélé, 2007: 29). As such, teacher education is seen neither primarily as the remit of teacher education institutions,

Table 7.1 Some aspects of global education reform trends and education policy principles in Finland since the 1980s

Global education reform trends	Education reform in Finland
Standardisation	Flexibility and loose standards
Setting clear, high and centrally prescribed performance standards for schools, teachers and students to improve the quality of outcomes.	Building on existing good practices and innovations in school-based curriculum development, setting of learning targets and networking through steering by information and support.
Focus on literacy and numeracy	Broad learning combined with creativity
Basic knowledge and skills in reading, writing, mathematics and natural sciences as prime targets of education reform.	Teaching and learning focus on deep and broad learning giving equal value to all aspects of an individual's growth in terms of personality, morality, creativity, knowledge and skills.
Consequential accountability	Intelligent accountability with trust-based professionalism
The school performance and the raising of student achievement are closely tied to the processes of promotion, inspection and ultimately rewarding or punishing schools and teachers based on accountability measures, especially standardised testing as the main criteria of success.	Adoption of intelligent accountability policies and gradual building of a culture of trust within the education system that values teachers' and headteachers' professionalism in judging what is best for students and in reporting their learning progress.

Source: Sahlberg, 2007

nor as a short-term initial teacher education endeavour, but as a more long-term professional journey encompassing initial teacher education, induction, early professional learning and subsequent continuing professional development (CPD). This reframing of teacher education in terms of location and duration has implications for educational leadership in schools and higher education institutions.

However, policy initiatives flowing directly from calls for a new, extended, higher-quality teacher professionalism may be problematic. Widespread evidence of this has been seen around the world, especially over the past decade. For example, the standardisation-focused globally dominant approach to educational reform (see Table 7.1) has manifested itself in changing patterns of teachers' work, including job intensification, decreasing resources, heightened surveillance and high-stakes testing of teachers and students, with damaging effects on the morale and learning of students, teachers, and communities, and consequently the role of education in promoting prosperous, just and equitable societies (Ball, 2003; Sachs, 2003; Dembélé and Schwille, 2006; Hargreaves, 2003; Sachs, 2008; Hargreaves, 2008). In some jurisdictions, however, the changing professional context of teachers' work has encompassed a deepening of professional knowledge, an increased scope for professional judgment, and richer, more cohesive and generative relationships with students, colleagues and the wider community (Hargreaves, 2008; Sahlberg, 2007). Finland, for example, has pursued an educational reform agenda over the past four decades centred on trust in teachers, vision and support for collegial professionalism, high-quality teacher education and limited use of high-stakes testing, that is, only at the end of post-primary education (Sahlberg, 2007).

As such, Finland's reforms have run counter to global education trends (see Table 7.1), which have focused on measuring, auditing, holding professionals to account in a technical, outcomes-driven way, and in communicating such outcomes in league tables (O'Brien and Brancaleone, 2010).

One of the central contradictions of the global emphasis on standardisation and high-stakes testing is that, despite a rhetoric emphasising the importance of standards, it actually undermines its own key goal of enhancing educational standards (Sachs, 2008). For example, Hargreaves (2008) has argued that intrusive, invasive and imposed school restructuring, as a response to failing schools, may prompt initial improvement to occur but long-term growth and renewal may not follow.

Why? Because the leadership qualities needed to turn around a school and bring about initial improvement may not be those that are essential for long-term capacity building. Hargreaves (2003) makes a strong case that teachers in a knowledge society need opportunities to become knowledgeable, inquiry-oriented professionals attentive to problems of practice and resourceful in identifying means of gathering appropriate evidence in order to foster a culture of knowledge generation and sharing in schools. The headline message here is clear: new understandings of quality teaching are prompting new ways of thinking about teachers' engagement with classroom practice and each other. Consequently, even comprehensive access by novice teachers to existing practice may not be sufficient to prepare them for changing understandings of teaching. For example, to what extent are NQTs in 2010 who are currently teaching secondary mathematics equipped to implement the new mathematics curriculum (Projects Maths)? Without adequate teacher support and appropriate leadership such an initiative is likely to result in 'innovation but no change'. We now turn to examining the ways in which visions of quality teacher education are putting pedagogy at the centre of teacher education.

Quality teacher education: promoting deep engagement with pedagogy in schools

> ... the work of teaching, like that of other professions, is viewed as non-routine and reciprocally related to learning; that is, what teachers do must be continually evaluated and reshaped based on whether it advances learning, rather than carried out largely by curriculum packages, scripts, and pacing schedules as many districts currently require. This means that teachers need highly refined knowledge and skills for assessing pupil learning, and they need a wide repertoire of practice – along with the knowledge to know when to use different strategies for different purposes.
>
> (Darling-Hammond, 2006: 394)

Frameworks for powerful teacher education have been advanced by a range of teacher educators over the past decade and increasingly highlight the central role of pedagogy (Brouwer and Korthagen, 2005; Darling-Hammond and Bransford, 2005; Darling-Hammond, 2006; Kennedy, 2005). We now focus on principles of quality teacher education drawn from the work of Darling-Hammond (2006: 6–18, 41–74), which we think is especially convincing as it involved a detailed comparative study of a number of initial teacher education programmes, that is, a comparison between seven reputed to be of high quality with a number of others. Drawing on multiple sources of evidence, Darling-Hammond and her colleagues undertook in-depth case studies of the seven highly regarded programmes, interviewing and surveying graduates and employers of the graduates (comparing them with a random comparison group of new teachers); observing the ITE programme practices as well as their graduates teaching in schools; and examining the module syllabi, assessments and the quality of teaching practice placements (2006: 7). Based on the in-depth case studies and comparative data, they identified a number of distinguishing features of those programmes reputed to be of high quality and summarised these in terms of design principles (see Box 7.1 and their elaboration below). Of particular relevance given our focus is the central role accorded to pedagogical knowledge, skills and understanding in the principles. So, for example, promoting student teachers' knowledge of learners (Principle 3), which might be taught in a psychology of education course, is optimal when linked to curriculum and pedagogy. Furthermore, pedagogy is given prominence in the principles emphasising professional standards/competences (Principle 2) and also in the integration of foundations, methods and teaching practice components of ITE (Principle 4).

Box 7.1   Principles of powerful teacher education

1 Vision
2 Focus on excellence in professional practice
3 Knowledge of learners linked to curriculum
4 Integration of foundations, methods and teaching practice
5 Addressing the apprenticeship of observation
6 Strategies to examine culture and schooling
7 Strong relationships, common knowledge and shared beliefs
8 Integration-focused projects

Source: Darling-Hammond, 2006

That is, what goes on inside the 'black box'[1] of teacher education –
be it in the university or school classroom spheres of ITE – matters in
highly significant ways. Drawing on and building upon Darling-
Hammond's (2006) synthesis of research on quality teacher education, the elaboration of the principles below provides valuable
guidance for leaders in the designing, reviewing and accrediting of
teacher education:

- Vision: a common, clear vision of good teaching practice integrated across course modules and teaching practice in schools;
- Focus on excellence in professional practice: clearly defined and
  agreed standards of 'good teaching' linked to wider professional
  standards;
- Knowledge of learners linked to curriculum: teaching of curriculum permeated by an understanding of the contingent nature of
  learning and the impact of both the immediate and wider social
  context on learning and teaching;
- Integration of foundations, methods and teaching practice: strategic initiatives to integrate foundations, curriculum/methods
  and teaching practice as the three core components of ITE;
- Addressing the apprenticeship of observation: given the long-
  term influence of the 15,000 hours student teachers have already
  spent in classrooms prior to entering ITE, there must be significant opportunity to make explicit the impact of these experiences on learning, teaching and curriculum;
- Strategies to examine culture and schooling: strategies to highlight the impact of culture (cultural homogeneity, diversity and
  change) in teacher education coursework and teaching practice;
- Strong relationships, common knowledge and shared beliefs:
  well-structured alliance between schools and universities built

around strong relationships, common knowledge and shared
beliefs to support ITE;

- Integration-focused projects: use of case studies, portfolios, per-
formances of understanding and other projects focused on supporting the integration of different knowledge sources on teaching,
learning and curriculum emerging from schools and universities.

An important point emerging from research on teacher education is
that processes and cultures within teacher education programmes
and their allied schools play a central role in mediating the quality
of learning experienced by student teachers in ITE (Haggar and
McIntyre, 2006; Darling-Hammond, 2006). For example, Tatto
(1999), based on a large-scale comprehensive empirical study of
teacher education programmes, provided strong evidence that con-
ceptions about pedagogy held by the teacher education staff, specifically concepts about teaching-related planning and decision-making
were associated with different teacher education programme designs
and learning outcomes for student teachers. That is, Tatto (1999)
observed how

> In programs where teaching was conceived, for the most part, as
> an externally regulated profession, teachers had few opportunities
> to understand, reflect on or align their practice in response to
> students' learning needs. In programs where teachers were seen
> as professional individuals capable of making informed instruc-
> tional choices, teachers had more opportunities to acquire the
> knowledge and skills to adjust instruction to learners' diverse
> needs. (Tatto, 1999: 95)

In this context, how schools and universities enact their roles in
teacher education, both in terms of structural arrangements and
cultural practices, has been the focus of considerable research over
the last decade. In the next section, we consider how the model of
university-school partnership as well as the culture of professional
learning in schools fosters or constrains a focus on pedagogy during
ITE and/or induction.

School-university partnerships and pedagogy

In this section, we address two aspects of school-university relationship
in terms of how they might deepen or limit a focus on pedagogy:
(i) models of school-university partnerships and (ii) the professional
learning culture in schools and the type of learning opportunities it
creates in ITE and/or induction.

Box 7.2   Five models of university-school partnerships in ITE (based on five-country cross-national study)

Model A: WORKPLACE/HOST MODEL

In this model, the school is the location where the student teacher undertakes a placement. The tertiary institution provides all coursework. This model typically involves some coaching by supervising teachers.

Model B: COORDINATOR MODEL

In this model, the school has a central supervisor or liaison teacher with the tertiary institution. This model is a variation on Model A. The difference is that in this model the school takes on the task of supervising student teachers by appointing an experienced colleague to coordinate teacher education.

Model C: PARTNER MODEL

A teacher in the school acts as a trainer of professional teachers. The school is partly responsible for the course curriculum. In addition to coaching the student teacher, the school also provides some of the training itself.

Model D: NETWORK MODEL

In this case, the trainer in the school is the leader of a training team in the school. The school is only partly responsible for the course curriculum. The school has a teacher education training team consisting of one or more trainers at school and coaches who are trained in teaching methods.

Model E: TRAINING SCHOOL MODEL

In this model, the entire training course is provided by the school. The tertiary institution functions as a backup or support institution, focusing on training the trainers at school and developing teaching and training methods.

Source: Maandag et al., 2007

First, the development of mentoring in schools in conjunction with university–school partnerships has become a key feature of redesigned teacher education over the past decade in many countries (OECD, 2005; Scottish Executive, 2004). It is common for formal partnership arrangements to be developed between higher education institutions and schools to provide structured support and a gradual increase in classroom responsibility for student teachers. The nature of such arrangements varies considerably (OECD, 2005; Maandag et al., 2007).

For example, Maandag et al. (2007) provide a useful framework (see Box 7.2) for characterising the nature of university–school collaboration. Based on a five-country cross-national study (England, France, Germany, the Netherlands and Sweden), they describe how these partnerships vary along a continuum from the school playing a host role (work placement model) to shared responsibility between the school and the higher education institute (partner model) to the school providing the entire training (training school model). In Ireland, school–higher education partnerships in ITE, we think, typically fall into the work placement model (i.e. A). The nature of the school–university relationship will doubtless impact the scope for a focus on pedagogy. However, the professional learning culture in schools, we think, is likely to be at least if not more influential in this regard. Consequently, in terms of cultures of professional learning in schools, we draw upon a large-scale study of induction in the USA, 'Project on the Next Generation of Teachers' (Moore-Johnson, 2004), which identified three school cultures vis-à-vis teacher learning that have very different implications for the types of support offered to newly qualified teachers. These researchers identified three school cultures which create very different learning opportunities for beginning teachers:

- novice-oriented professional culture: beginner teachers support each other with little or no mentoring including opportunities to observe and share practice;
- experienced/veteran-oriented professional culture: experienced/veteran teachers are supportive in a general way, yet by and large provide no mentoring, observation opportunities or feedback on classroom teaching;
- integrated professional culture: learning to teach is seen as a task for all in the school. Support for newly qualified teachers (NQTs) was generally widespread across the school with peer observation, feedback and a coaching culture centred around sharing professional practice and a deep focus on pedagogy.

Any of the five models, albeit within that model's parameters, might provide significantly different support and access to practice for student teachers or NQTs. Of particular significance in relation to opportunities to see, understand, share and develop pedagogy is that only in the integrated professional learning culture were NQTs in a position to engage deeply and collaboratively with pedagogy – both their own and that of other teachers.

In this context, we note findings based on a recent study of a postgraduate secondary teacher education programme, *Learning to*

Teach Study (LETS: Conway, et al., 2010a), which found that only a minority of ITE students actually had opportunities to observe another teacher teach during the entire course of the programme. Furthermore, there appeared to be quite different school cultures underpinning the practice of observing and giving feedback to PGDE students in schools, with some students experiencing considerable support and others minimal. However, even for those who experienced considerable support this typically did not extend so far as to involve deep engagement with pedagogy in terms of co-planning, co-teaching, being observed and getting feedback as well as observing accomplished teachers. The LETS findings are consistent with the recent TALIS findings.

Some guidelines on promoting deeper engagement with pedagogy

Looking and seeing in classrooms: peer observation and insight

Providing student teachers and NQTs with observation opportunities alone is unlikely to be sufficient in providing access to the practice of teaching, for a number of reasons. First, research on differences between the observation patterns of novice compared with expert[2] teachers convincingly demonstrates that there are very significant differences in what is 'seen' of classroom life – despite the 'same' observation opportunities (Berliner, 2004). Berliner (2004) noted, in his review of two decades of novice–expert research on teaching, that expert or accomplished teachers' understanding and representation of classroom problems is very different from that of novices, and that they also have very fast and accurate pattern recognition of classroom dynamics (for example, they are able to identify students who are struggling or situations likely to cause classroom management problems). Second, in arguing for deeper engagement with pedagogy, we see this is a necessary but not sufficient condition to broaden student teachers' and NQTs' horizons of observation. Student teachers need to be supported in this process by also having ways of talking with accomplished teachers whose teaching they observe (Zanting et al., 2001; Haggar and McIntyre, 2006). Similarly, teachers being observed also need support in being able to 'uncover practice', that is their planning, actual teaching as well as post-lesson reflections, for newcomers to the profession (Zanting et al., 2001; Lieberman and Pointer Mace, 2009; Haggar and McIntyre, 2006). Third, the range of observation opportunities and associated conversations about practice need to be specific to particular tasks and practices in teaching. Why? Because compared with novices, who find it difficult to make sense of complex classroom situations, expert teachers are adept at noticing patterns in specific areas in which they have extensive experience, that is, they possess expertise that is very domain-specific. For example, an experienced primary classroom teacher may have a different pattern recognition capacity from that of a subject teacher at post-primary level. Similarly, pattern recognition may differ for teachers of different subjects, as their expertise depends on their subject knowledge, among other things.

Sharing and talking about practice: the 'Why didn't you?' question

Given the new regulations for ITE signed by the Minister for Education and Skills in November 2009, second level ITE students are now required to have observation opportunities in their teaching practice schools. Parenthetically, it is curious why this was not also made a requirement for primary level teacher education – possibly because this is more likely to occur in the concurrent-model-dominated primary teacher education sector. As observation is never far from judgment of others' practice, how can what might be seen as a relatively threatening professional experience be structured as a generative one for all involved? An illuminating example is the recent research study on the dynamics of teaching practice in schools by Haggar and McIntyre, in which student teachers were banned from asking practising teachers 'Why didn't you?' after observing lessons (Haggar and McIntyre, 2006). That is, student teachers were *not* permitted to use this question, following observations of their cooperating teachers, because it evoked anxiety and defensiveness even among experienced teachers with whom they were paired. As such, availing of the lessons from experienced teachers demanded a particular professional lexicon and a sensitivity to the cultural dynamic in which the act of teaching is seen as very personal – and typically not open to observation. As Shulman (1993) noted, when we enter the classroom we enter the world of 'pedagogical solitude' rather than a space in which teaching can be shared in a collegial context, that is, where teaching is viewed as community property. The lesson from the 'Why didn't you?' decision is informative, in that it highlights how evaluation is always barely beneath the surface in any observation encounter in classrooms, whether this is between experienced teachers on home turf and student teachers as 'visiting observers' in their classrooms, or indeed visits by tutors on teaching practice supervisions.

Matters of representation: profiles and portfolios of practice in classrooms

In efforts to promote greater coherence and knowledge integration in ITE, the long-espoused reflective practice model (evident since the mid 1980s) is increasingly being complemented by an emphasis on promoting an inquiry stance in student teachers (Lyons, 2010; Rath, 2009, 2010), for example, use of portfolios (in the USA in particular) and completion of a substantial research thesis as part of a master's degree for initial teacher certification. (In Finland ITE involves completion of a master's degree, OECD, 2005; Conway et al., 2009.) However, portfolios of teaching practice undertaken by ITE students and/or NQTs also need to be complemented and extended by profiles of practice that provide insights on the particular scripts that shape practice. For example, Lyons et al.'s (2003) video study – *Inside Classrooms* – of mathematics and English teaching in Junior Cycle (12–15-year-olds) provides powerful insights on the dominant pedagogical approaches that might be invisible to newcomers or indeed experienced teachers were it not for the power of comprehensive analysis of classroom discourse undertaken by educational researchers. Their study was able to demonstrate that 92 per cent of talk in classrooms was undertaken by teachers, significantly foreclosing on students' learning opportunities.

Our point here is that as new visions of what counts as good teaching practice emerge (for example, Project Maths in second level schools or new initiatives in any other curricular area), the access to practice and focus on pedagogy – which we see as crucial for quality teacher education – must be informed by different representations of good practice. For example, a digital video recreation of the prototypical maths lessons observed in the *Inside Classrooms* study could be a powerful professional learning tool to help new and accomplished teachers understand existing practice as they consider how they might adapt their practice in light of new curricular visions of good mathematics teaching (NCCA, 2005; Conway and Sloane, 2006). Crucially, deepening engagement with pedagogy clearly involves student teachers and NQTs having access to lesson observations and associated conversations with accomplished teachers, but it also means that all teachers need access to multiple representations of practice (for example, portfolios, videos) that will mediate their own understandings of these practices.

Engaging with pedagogy and models of school–university partnership

New learning identities are shaped by the participation structures afforded to learners (Wenger, 2008; Hall et al., 2008). The strategic building of learning partnerships between universities and schools is essential for generating a framework for new modes of professional engagement, participation, lifelong learning and creating the kind of structures that synergistically prepare teachers for active engagement in shaping the 21st-century professional (Scottish Executive, 2004; Wilson et al., 2006). Learning to teach involves preparation for not only life in the classroom but also active engagement in teaching as a professional learning community – with, as we have made a case for in this chapter, deeper engagement with pedagogy.

Learning to teach occurs best when undertaken as a form of assisted practice (rather than solo practice). This has significant implications for school–university partnerships in terms of how teaching practice and school experiences are structured. They must provide opportunities for observation of, and conversation with, experienced teachers in light of the reform-oriented teaching being advocated at a national level (for example, Revised Primary School Curriculum; developments at Junior and Senior Cycle, Murphy, 2004; Looney and Klenowski, 2008).

Teachers have potentially an even more crucial role in the induction phase of learning to teach. Exemplary induction programmes recognise the strengths and potentials of the different contexts of learning to teach. The National Pilot Project on Teacher Induction (NPPTI) (Killeavy and Murphy, 2006a, 2006b) is one example of this kind of partnership in action. It recognised that beginning teachers need support in their first year of full-time teaching, and also offered professional development for the experienced teachers in participating schools who took on a formal mentoring role for beginner teachers. It is unfortunate that the potential role of school-based mentors for pre-service teachers has not yet been addressed in a similar way.

During teaching practice, the messages about good teaching that the student teacher receives from foundation and teaching studies courses and from university lecturers and tutors are tested out, evaluated, internalised and put into operation. The student's task of forming a coherent professional identity is naturally more straightforward and generative when both contexts are largely in agreement about the role of the teacher and what good teaching is, or what Tatto (1999) calls 'normative cohesion', than if there are conflicting messages coming from each setting. In many countries, new understandings of the optimal conditions for learning to teach – during ITE and induction in the context of university–school partnerships – have created a new appreciation of teachers as school-based teacher educators and highlighted the need to foster close relationships with university-based teacher educators (Byrne, 2002; Feiman-Nemser, 2001; Furlong et al., 2008; OECD, 2005; Commonwealth Schools

Commission, 2007). According to Lieberman and Pointer Mace (2009: 460) the distinguishing feature of accomplished teachers is that 'they can deconstruct their practice, explain it to others, and in the process learn how to facilitate learning for (and with) their peers', by inviting them into dialogue around 'see how we teach'. Creating opportunities for such dialogue both within the school and with colleagues from other schools and from teacher education institutions is essential. Partnership with a higher education institution offers teachers opportunities both to update their knowledge and to engage in this kind of professional dialogue, which is essential for ongoing professional development. Participation by teachers in an initial teacher education partnership not only offers opportunities for ongoing professional development for those involved but also enhances the whole school as a community of learners, entailing as it does the development of a shared professional language for talking about teaching and learning (Pollard and Newman, 2009). The involvement of teachers in the university-based components of ITE can also be enriching, connecting the students directly to current issues of pedagogy and practice.

Moving away from the current workplace/host model (see Box 7.2 above) towards this kind of partner or network model has implications for the way that ITE at both primary and post-primary levels is currently structured. A necessary prerequisite would be the establishment of formal partnership arrangements which specify the roles and responsibilities of schools and higher education institutions in providing structured support and a gradual increase in classroom responsibility for student teachers (as recommended by the Byrne Report, 2002). Structured support would include providing opportunities for observing teachers, planning and discussing lessons and undertaking assignments with the appropriate and necessary ethical considerations addressed. Teachers might be involved in discussions around selecting topics for projects and portfolio entries, as well as on subject-specific pedagogy. This would of course have implications for resourcing and timetabling; in many other countries mentor teachers have timetabled hours for this work (Conway et al., 2009). Professional development for mentor teachers is also essential, both as part of their continuing professional development and as a recognition of their position as leaders within the profession, either through titles such as Chartered Teacher (Scotland) or through the award of additional professional qualifications (for example, as an option within a Masters course, or a more specialised qualification such as the Graduate Certificate/MEd in Educational Mentoring at the University of Limerick or the Graduate Certificate in Mentoring and Coaching offered by the University of Tasmania, Conway et al., 2009).

Conclusion: teaching, solitude and community property

Policy interest in teacher education in Ireland has been more intense in Ireland over the past decade (2001–10) compared with the previous decade (Byrne, 2002; Kellaghan, 2002; Coolahan, 2003; Burke, 2003; Egan, 2006; Drudy, 2006; Coolahan, 2007; Dolan and Gleeson, 2007; Conway et al., 2009; Killeavy and Murphy, 2006a; Harford, 2010). Various reports, studies and commentaries have signalled the need to strengthen teacher learning across the professional continuum. Significantly, these documents point to how the duration and location of teacher education has changed with implications for leaders at all levels of the education system. In Ireland, as in many other countries, the reconfiguration of teacher education is posing challenges for what Shulman (1993) terms the culture of 'pedagogical solitude' that is typically dominant in schools. In this chapter, we have made a case for a deepening of engagement with pedagogy as a key issue for leadership in teacher education at a time of significant review and reform in teacher education in Ireland. Deepening engagement with pedagogy implies a cultural shift from the dominance of the teachers' legendary autonomy to the cultivation of teaching as community property – notwithstanding a certain inescapable and necessary solitude in teaching. Deepening engagement with pedagogy demands a multidimensional and multi-level approach to re-culture the opportunities for learning to teach in ITE and induction including observation, co-planning, co-teaching, representations of existing and reform-oriented images of teaching (that is, preferably both in text format as well as case examples on digital video). The principle of fostering a perspective on teaching as community property is, we think, vital, and potentially generative, at a time when teacher education is undergoing review encompassing the Teaching Council's specification of teacher competences as well as its piloting of a teacher education programme accreditation system in 2009–10 and associated initiatives to enhance teacher learning across the professional continuum. A number of initiatives and research studies in Ireland over the past few years provide insights on the dynamics of deepening engagement with pedagogy. Among these are the following:

- lesson study projects in which teachers collaboratively plan and reflect on teaching co-planned lessons using digital video and other artefacts to illustrate their practice for others (for example, Kelly and Sloane, 2003; Leavy, 2009; Corcoran, 2008);
- team teaching initiatives (for example, O'Murchú, 2009);

- the use of digital video of lessons as a context for developing practice in post-primary ITE (Harford et al., 2010), and among primary teachers on literacy and ICT projects (Conway et al., 2010b);
- lesson lab to enhance teachers' practice in primary mathematics during which an accomplished teacher teaches for a group of colleagues and the digital video of the lesson is used for subsequent discussion – similar to lesson study noted above (Delaney et al., 2010).

All these projects in various ways are 'uncovering practice' for peers and providing insight into pedagogy through modelling, sharing and discussion. Such projects will be useful in considering how leaders at various levels who take responsibility for the profession of teaching must involve the professionals themselves in collaboration with colleges and universities and lead/leader professionals. Consequently, the profession will need to play a more interventionist role in the future in order to foster what the TALIS report termed 'more complex professional collaboration' (Gilleece et al., 2009). The maturity of the teaching profession is, arguably, in proportion to the extent to which it can play a significant role in the enculturation of new entrants to the profession. School leaders, it seems, are pivotal in this regard since they are the ones best equipped to understand the intricacies and complexities of pedagogy, curriculum design, programme and curriculum evaluation, assessment and classroom management. It is to such people that beginner teachers look to articulate, communicate and demonstrate fine-grained details and analyses of these elements of teaching and learning. Most significantly, leaders need to include in their repertoire of responsibilities a concern for the beginner teacher and a recognition that learning to teach is not the sole function of the individual beginner teacher but also a function of the more established professional, especially those in positions of leadership.

Notes

1   In 1998 Paul Black and Dylan Wiliam likened the classroom to a 'black box', since initiatives tended to focus on inputs and outputs, not on what went on inside it.
2   Growing out of hundreds of novice–expert studies examining the development of expertise in a wide range of fields (e.g. medicine, chess, golf), this research points to a number of consequential features that distinguish novices from experts (Berliner, 2004; Bransford et al., 2005).

References

Ball, S. (2003) 'The teacher's soul and the terrors of performativity', *Journal of Education Policy*, 18(2): 215–28.

Barber, M. and Mourshed, M. (2007) *How the World's Best Performing School Systems Come Out in Top (McKinsey Report)*. Retrieved June 2008 from www.mckinsey.com/clientservice/socialsector/resources/pdf/Worlds_School_Systems_Final.pdf

Black, P. and Wiliam, D. (1998) *Inside the Black Box: Raising Standards through Classroom Assessment*. London: King's College.

Berliner, D.C. (2004) 'Describing the behaviour and documenting the accomplishments of expert teachers', *Bulletin of Science, Technology and Society*, 24(3): 200–212.

Bransford, J., Darling-Hammond, L. and Pamela LePage, P. (2005) 'Introduction', in L. Darling-Hammond, L. and J. Bransford (eds), *Preparing Teachers for a Changing World: What Teachers Should Learn and be Able to Do*. San Francisco: Jossey Bass.

Brouwer, N., and Korthagen, F. (2005) 'Can teacher education make a difference?', *American Educational Research Journal*, 42(1): 153–224.

Burke, A. (2003) 'Report on second north south conference on initial teacher education', in A. Pollak (ed.), *Challenges to Teacher Education North and South* (SCoTENS Annual Report 2003), 77–9. Armagh: Centre for Cross Border Studies.

Byrne, K. (2002) *Advisory Group on Post-Primary Teacher Education*. Dublin: Department of Education and Science.

Commonwealth Schools Commission (2007) *Top of the Class: Report on the Inquiry into Teacher Education*. Canberra: Commonwealth of Australia.

Conway, P.F. (2010) 'Learning to teach: metaphors, other professions and horizons of observation'. Presidential Address at the Educational Studies Association of Ireland (ESAI) Annual Conference, Dundalk, 26 March.

Conway, P.F. and Sloane, F.C. (2006) *International Trends in Post-primary Mathematics Education: Perspectives on Learning, Teaching and Assessment*. Dublin: NCCA.

Conway, P.F., Murphy, R., Rath, A. and Hall, K. (2009) *Learning to Teach and Its Implications for the Continuum of Teacher Education: A Nine-Country Cross National Study*. Report commissioned by the Teaching Council, Ireland. www.teachingcouncil.ie

Conway, P.F., Murphy, R., Delargey, M., Hall, K., Kitching, K., Long, F., McKeon, J., Murphy, B., O'Brien, S. and O'Sullivan, D. (2010a) *Learning to Teach Study (LETS): Developing Curricular and Cross-curricular Competences in Becoming a 'Good' Secondary Teacher*. Unpublished report. Cork: School of Education, UCC.

Conway, P.F., Murphy, R. and Rath, A. (2010b) *Literacy and ICT Project: Final Evaluation Report*. Dublin: National Centre for Technology Education.

Coolahan, J. (2003). *Attracting, Developing and Retaining Effective Teachers: Country Background Report for Ireland*. Dublin: Department of Education and Science.

Coolahan, J. (2007) 'The operational environment for future planning in teacher education: OECD and EU Initiatives', in R. Dolan and J. Gleeson (eds), *The Competences Approach to Teacher Professional Development: Current Practice and Future Prospects* (SCoTENS Annual Report 2007). Armagh: Centre for Cross Border Studies.

Corcoran, D. (2008) 'Learning to teach mathematics using Japanese lesson study: A case in Ireland', in O. Figueras, J.L. Cortina, S. Alatorre, T. Rojano and

A. Sepulveda (eds), *Proceedings of the Joint Meeting of PME 32 and PME-NA XXX (Vol. 1: 250). Mexico: Cinvestav-UMSNH.*

Darling-Hammond, L. (2006). *Powerful Teacher Education: Lessons from Exemplary Programs*. San Francisco: Jossey-Bass.

Darling-Hammond, L. and Bransford, J. (eds) (2005) *Preparing Teachers for a Changing World: What Teachers Should Learn and Be Able to Do*. Washington: US National Academy of Education.

Delaney, S., Corcoran, D. and Leavy, A. (2010) 'Mathematics teaching as an activity and an object of study'. Paper presented at the annual conference of the American Educational Research Association (AERA), Denver, April.

Dembélé, M. and Schwille, J. (2006) 'Can the global trend toward accountability be reconciled with ideals of teacher empowerment?: Theory and Practice in Guinea', *International Journal of Educational Research*, 45(4–5): 302–14.

Dolan, R. and Gleeson, J. (eds) (2007) *The Competences Approach to Teacher Professional Development: Current Practice and Future Prospects* (SCoTENS Annual Report). Armagh: Centre for Cross Border Studies.

Drudy, S. (2006) 'Change and reform in teacher education in Ireland: A case study in the reform of higher education', in P. Zgaga (ed.), *Modernization of Study Programmes in Teachers' Education in an International Context*. Retrieved from www.pef.uni-lj.si/bologna/dokumenti/posvet-drudy.pdf

Egan, E. (2006) 'Key messages on teacher education', in A. Pollak (ed.), *Teacher Education and Schools: Together Towards Improvement* (SCoTENS Annual Report 2006: 52–9). Armagh: Centre for Cross Border Studies.

Feiman-Nemser, S. (2001) 'From preparation to practice: Designing a continuum to strengthen and sustain teaching', *Teachers College Record*, 103(6): 1013–55.

Furlong, J., Cochran Smith, M. and Brennan, M. (2008) 'Politics, Policy and Teacher Education; Introduction', in J. Furlong, M. Cochran Smith and M. Brennan (eds), special edition of *Teachers and Teaching: Theory and Practice on Politics and Policy in Teacher Education: International Perspectives*, 14(4): 265–9.

Gilleece, L., Shiel, G., Perkins, R. with Proctor, M. (2009) *Teaching and Learning International Survey. National Report for Ireland*. Dublin: Educational Research Centre.

Haggar, H. and McIntyre, D. (2006) *Learning Teaching from Teachers: Realising the Potential of School-based Teacher Education*. Buckingham: Open University Press.

Hall, K., Murphy, P. and Soler, J. (2008) *Pedagogy and Practice: Culture and Identities*. London: Sage Publications/The Open University.

Harford, J. (2010) 'Teacher education policy in Ireland and the challenges of the 21st century', *European Journal of Teacher Education*, 33(4).

Harford, J., MacRuairc., G. and McCartan, D. (2010) 'Lights, camera, reflection: Using peer video to promote dialogue among student teachers', *Teacher Development*, 14(1): 57–68.

Hargreaves, A. (2003) *Teaching in the Knowledge Society*. Buckingham: Open University Press.

Hargreaves, A. (2008) 'The coming of post-standardization: three weddings and a funeral', in C. Sugrue (ed.), *The Future of Educational Change: International Perspectives*. London and New York: Routledge.

Howey, K.R. and Zimpher, N.L. (1999) 'Pervasive problems and issues in teacher education', in G.A. Griffin (ed.), *The Education of Teachers (Ninety-eighth Yearbook of the National Society for the Study of Education, Part I)*, (pp. 279–305). Chicago, IL: University of Chicago Press.

Hutchins, E. (1993) 'Learning to navigate', in S. Chaiklin and J. Lave (eds), *Understanding Practice*. New York: Cambridge University Press.

Kellaghan, T. (2002) *Preparing Teachers for the 21st Century: Report of the Working Group on Primary Preservice Teacher Education*. Dublin: Department of Education and Science.

Kelly, A. and Sloane, F. (2003) 'Educational research and the problems of practice', *Irish Educational Studies*, 22(1): 29–40.

Kennedy, M. (2005) *Inside Teaching: How Classroom Life Undermines Reform*. Cambridge: Harvard University Press.

Killeavy, M. and Murphy, R. (2006a) *National Pilot Project on Teacher Induction: Report on Phase 1 and 2, 2002–2005*. Dublin: Department of Education and Science.

Killeavy, M. and Murphy, R. (2006b) 'Partnership in teacher induction: The teacher induction pilot project', in A. Pollak (ed.), *Teacher Education and Schools: Together Towards Improvement* (SCoTENS Annual Report 2006: 63–7). Armagh: Centre for Cross Border Studies.

Lave, J. and Wenger, E. (1991) *Situated Learning: Legitimate Peripheral Participation*. Cambridge: Cambridge University Press.

Lave, J. and Wenger, E. (1998) *Communities of Practice: Learning, Meaning, and Identity*. Cambridge: Cambridge University Press.

Leavy, A.M. (2009) 'A picture is worth a thousand words: Insights into graphicacy skills of primary preservice teachers', in S. Close, T. Dooley and D. Corcoran (eds), *Proceedings of the Second National Conference on Research on Mathematics Education in Ireland – MEI II*. Dublin: St Patrick's College.

Lieberman, A. and Pointer Mace, D.H. (2009) 'The role of ' accomplished teachers' in professional learning communities: uncovering practice and enabling leadership', *Teachers and Teaching: Theory and Practice*, 15(4): 459–70.

Looney, A. and Klenowski, V. (2008) 'Curriculum and assessment for the knowledge society: interrogating experiences in the Republic of Ireland and Queensland, Australia', *Curriculum Journal*, 19(3): 177–92.

Lyons, M., Lynch, K., Close, S., Sheerin, E. and Boland, P. (2003) *Inside Classrooms: the Teaching and Learning of Mathematics in Social Context*. Dublin: IPA.

Lyons, N. (ed.) (2010) *The Handbook on Reflective Inquiry*, Amsterdam: Springer Press.

Maandag, D.W, Deinum, J.F.,Hofman, A. and Buitink, J. (2007) 'Teacher education in schools: an international comparison', *European Journal of Teacher Education*, 30(2): 151–73.

Moore-Johnson, S. (2004) *Finders and Keepers: Helping New Teachers Survive and Thrive in Our Schools*. San Francisco: Jossey Bass.

Moreno, J.M. (2005) *Learning to Teach in the Knowledge Society: Final Report*. Washington: World Bank.

Murphy, B. (2004) 'Social interaction and language use in Irish infant classrooms in the context of the revised Irish Primary School Curriculum', *Literacy*, 38(3): 149–55.

NCCA (2005) *Review of Mathematics in Post-Primary Education*. Dublin: National Council for Curriculum and Assessment.

O'Brien, S. and Brancaleone, D. (2010) 'Evaluating learning outcomes: In search of lost knowledge', *Irish Educational Studies*.

O'Murchú, F. (2009) 'Team teaching: Supporting student and teacher learning in post-primary classrooms', *Learn*, 31: 88–106.

OECD (2005) *Teachers Matter: Attracting, Retaining and Developing Teachers*. Paris: OECD.

OECD/LDS (2007) *Improving School Leadership. OECD Project Background Report – Ireland*. Accessed at http://www.oecd.org/edu/schoolleadership.

Pollard, Andrew and Newman, Mark (2009) *Educational Research: A Foundation for Teacher Professionalism?* In: The Routledge Education Studies Textbook. Routledge, Abingdon.

Rath, A. (2009) 'Creating Learning Communities: An Interrogation of a Sustainable professional development model', in C.J.Craig, and Deretchin, P. (eds) *Teacher Educators Yearbook XV11*, Maryland: Rowman & Littlefield:

Rath, A. (2010) 'Reflective practice as conscious geometry: portfolios as a tool for sponsoring, scaffolding and assessing reflective inquiry in learning to teach', in N.Lyons, (ed.) *The Handbook on Reflective Inquiry*. Amsterdam: Springer Press.

Sachs, J. (2003) 'Teacher professional standards: controlling or developing teaching?', *Teachers and Teaching: Theory and Practice*, 9(2): 175–86.

Sachs, J. (2008) 'The knowledge society as a trigger for change in contemporary educational policy and practice', in Sugrue, C. (ed.) *The Future of Educational Change: International Perspectives*. London:Routledge/Taylor & Francis.

Sahlberg, P. (2007) 'Education policies for raising student learning: the Finnish approach', *Journal of Education Policy*, 22(2): 147–71.

Scottish Executive (2004) *Building the Foundations of a Lifelong Learning Society: A Review of Collaboration Between Schools and Further Education Colleges in Scotland*. Edinburgh: Scottish Executive.

Schwille, J. and Dembélé, M. (2007) *Global Perspectives on Teacher Learning: Improving Policy and Practice*. Paris: UNESCO.

Shulman, L.S. (1993) 'Teaching as community property: Putting an end to pedagogical solitude'. *Change*, Nov. 1993: 6–7.

Tatto, T. (1999) 'The socializing influence of normative cohesive teacher education on teachers' beliefs about instructional choice', *Teachers and Teaching*, 5(1): 95–118.

UNESCO (2005) *Education for All: The Quality Imperative*. Available at http://www.unesco.org/en/efareport/reports/2005-quality/

Wenger, E. (2008) 'Identity in Practice', in K. Hall, P. Murphy and J. Soler (eds) *Pedagogy and Practice: Culture and Identities*, pp. 105–14. London: Sage.

Wilson, V., Hall, J., Davidson, J. and Lewin, J. (2006) *Developing Teachers: A Review of Early Professional Learning: Full Report*. Edinburgh: General Teaching Council Scotland.

Zanting, A., Verloop, N., and Vermunt, J. (2001) 'Student teachers eliciting mentors' practical knowledge and comparing it to their own beliefs', *Teaching and Teacher Education*, 17(6): 725–740.

Chapter 8

Leading and Managing Professional Learning in Schools

Helen O'Sullivan

Abstract

Developing schools where the professionals are engaged in ongoing learning based on critical appraisal of their practice with a view to improvement is a challenging responsibility for school leaders and managers. This chapter is the story of a case study of one such undertaking in an Irish primary school. The chapter is based on the premise that for professional development to lead to real, enhanced learning for students and teachers, schools must incorporate the systems and procedures to facilitate embedding learning in practice. This involves working at different levels in schools, at classroom level to change practice, at whole staff level to change perceptions and at organisational level to change structures. Unless such changes are supported by informed and professionally challenging facilitation the effects will be limited.

Key words/phrases

Professional learning community; collaborative practice; leadership and school-based professional development; quality teaching and learning; building in-school capacity; teacher professional development; changing teachers' practice.

Introduction

Teacher professional development is an issue that preoccupies the attention of those involved in education systems across the globe. This preoccupation has recently become more intense as research evidence continues to emphasise that teacher-learning to improve practice is the single most powerful leverage in providing quality learning and teaching (Barber and Mourshed, 2007). The evidence also shows that if such professional learning is to lead to changing practice it is most effective when based on-site, in schools, and close to the daily interactions between teachers, students and the learning content. The concept of the school as a professional learning community (PLC) is most frequently promoted as the context to facilitate such professional learning. There is now a growing body of research that supports the PLC concept. However, knowing *that* the PLC school is an effective model to advance professional learning to change practice is different from knowing *how* this can be realised in schools. In Ireland there are scant examples of such schools. Leading and managing in-school professional learning within the framework of the PLC concept is the focus of this chapter.

The chapter is in three parts. Part one considers the dominant context of professional development in Ireland. Part two tells the research story upon which the chapter is based. In part three the learning from the research is examined in the light of the context described. The heart of the matter is the story of a two-year action research inquiry into the facilitation of teachers' school-based professional learning to change practice. The author, as external facilitator, led an in-school professional learning programme to improve the quality of teaching and learning of writing, within the English curriculum, in a primary school in Ireland. The focus was on developing systems and procedures for learning through sharing practice, leading to improved classroom experiences for students and teachers. This story highlights a range of issues that emerge when teachers and school leaders in Ireland attempt to change culture and practice within a national teaching environment where isolated practice still predominates and no formal systems of feedback are generally practised. Integral to the intervention was the building of in-school capacity to lead its own professional development programme in the future.

The prelude

The story of teacher professional development in Ireland reflects a 'chequered history' (Coolahan, 2007: 2). Coolahan describes that history as periods of activity and flourishing followed by periods of retrenchment. From that perspective, the past decade (1999–2009) was a period of flourishing while current indicators are that we are facing into a period of retrenchment. From 1999 onwards the establishment of in-service programmes (at one point over 30 in number), organised on a national basis and designed and delivered by teachers seconded from their schools, became the normative response to professional development needs. It would seem that the dominant vision of teacher professional development was that it is the responsibility of the Department of Education and Skills (DES) to provide professional development and that that provision be peer-led, during school time based on withdrawing teachers from school. The purpose of the majority of the initiatives was to drive through curricular change and implement school planning. It was presumed that by attending seminars and workshops teachers would then implement the externally determined goals in their daily practice. There were some examples of follow-up in-school support, the effectiveness of which is still to be assessed. Towards the end of that decade there were some initiatives that indicated a growing awareness of the need to change the approach (Project Maths, for example). With a focus on curricular implementation, based on intensive input over selected off-site days, it is not surprising that an evaluation of one of the primary curriculum support programmes found that after five years of intensive in-service, with the exception of planning, there was little evidence of increases in teacher and school capability to advance their own teaching and learning processes (Loxley et al., 2007).

Sugrue (2002) highlighted that the Irish model resulted not only in very fragmented experience for teachers, but also in an experience of professional learning that is limiting. Sugrue suggests that when knowledge is presented as coming from the expert in compliance with a given policy, without 'appropriate support and context sensitive feedback' (Sugrue, 2002: 318) teachers apply their new skills without questioning and devoid of critical examination.

The in-service model has its detractors worldwide. Joyce and Showers (2002) emphasise the limitations of off-site professional development when used in isolation. They also claim that the difficulties in transferring and implementing new learning to the classroom are a 'product of weak preservice and inservice programs, not in the learning ability of teachers' (Joyce and Showers, 2002: 3). Like Sugrue, they too insist that without school-based learning through feedback and coaching few professionals use new strategies until they become normative practices.

It is my thesis that, in the spirit of the 1991 OECD report, there should be a variety of pathways to professional development, but that all programmes must have the expectation of improving learning outcomes in schools – student and adult. In respecting the professionalism of the teaching body and in the interest of sustainability, such programmes should also include building each school's capacity to advance their own teaching and learning processes through teacher agency. Therefore, given the weight of evidence, all programmes must sooner or later be brought back to the school setting for the practice, feedback and embedding into practice that is critical for change. In order for that to happen, schools must develop the structures and capacities to become professional learning communities (McLaughlin and Talbert, 2006). By professional learning communities is meant schools that are actively engaged in critical examination of the values that underpin their practice, creating the conditions for sharing leadership, taking collective responsibility for all pupils' learning guided by ongoing monitoring and assessment. As quoted in Stoll et al. (2006), a professional learning community is:

> ... an inclusive group of people, motivated by a shared learning vision, who support and work with each other, finding ways inside and outside their immediate community, to enquire into their own practice and together learn new and better approaches that will enhance all pupils' learning. (Stoll, 2006: 6)

Creating professional learning community schools is a complex undertaking, as research has identified because 'when we turn to the school level ... we run into a series of structural, cultural, and vocational impediments' (Grossman et al., 2000: 10). In the Irish context it is deemed particularly challenging given our dominant culture of non-interference with professionals.

Given that teachers differ in terms of knowledge, skills, dispositions/willingness to change, leading and managing whole school improvement as outlined above is not simple. However, the undeniable evidence that in-school variability in the quality of teaching is a real problem and has to be tackled (Konstantopoulos, 2006; Barber and Mourshed, 2007) means that school leaders, when trying to improve school practice, cannot simply work with volunteers alone, as perhaps researchers can. Thus there are implications in terms of approach and pacing. As an occasional hill walker I draw an analogy with the guide leading a large group of walkers of varying levels of experience and fitness on a new route: the guide has the responsibility to choose a route within everyone's capability, and must constantly check that those out front don't advance so far ahead as to lose those falling behind. The group still arrives at its destination! However, my experience has been that when inter-group interaction is nurtured, people change walking partners as they go, they connect, develop mutual appreciation and trust, the pace tends to settle, and they are more likely to walk again as a group. In fact, the likelihood is they choose an even more challenging route next time.

The purpose of this research was threefold: to improve the teaching and learning of writing in the school; to build the school's own capacity to lead its own professional learning in the future; and to learn about facilitating school-based professional learning within the framework of a professional learning community. The third purpose is the subject of this chapter.

The story

I have used the terms 'professional development' and 'professional learning' somewhat interchangeably. However, at this point I make a distinction between them. Teachers' experience of professional development in Ireland has not necessarily resulted in deep professional learning to change practice even in the targeted areas (NCCA, 2008). Professional development has come to be synonymous with DES-led initiatives that teachers are expected to attend. The research that is the focus of this chapter is about developing in-school initiatives to improve practice that is henceforth referred to as professional learning.

The research school is a 24-teacher (18 mainstream, five learning support and principal), urban boys' primary school in Ireland. A senior primary school, the pupils range approximately from six to seven years of age (first class) to 12 or 13 (sixth class). While the school has an open admissions policy, its catchment area would be considered predominantly middle class in character. The staff ratio of male to female is 7:17. At the time of the research 13 teachers were under 35 years of age while 11 were over thirty-five.

The intervention involved setting up structures and process to facilitate the school's functioning as a professional learning community with a single focus of improving the teaching and learning of writing. Having a single focus greatly helped in that all efforts converged in learning together for a shared purpose. This was done mainly through facilitating teachers 'acting' their way into understanding by providing them 'with experiences that allowed them to begin functioning as a professional learning community' (Burnette, 2002: 2). In terms of the structures, the intervention was team based, all teachers in the school participated in a learning team: six three-teacher professional learning teams (TPLTs) were established, each including one facilitator and, in this case, corresponding to class levels in the school. These teams met about six times during each year. It was the intention to meet monthly but in practice this did not always work out. Due to the 'busyness' of school life and the contingency nature of freeing up in-school time, the TPLT teams met on average six or seven times each year. The researcher met the facilitators' team (FT). Meetings of the FT team did take place as planned mainly due to the fact that they were scheduled as early morning meetings for one hour prior to school commencement. The FT met to co-design and model each new TPLT meeting involving collective reflection, learning and taking direction from the previous month's experience. It was the responsibility of the school leadership to free up time for meetings. School leadership also provided practical and financial support through engaging outside expertise when needed. The teachers, together with the external facilitator, monitored ongoing effectiveness. Effectiveness was determined by the extent to which the teachers' engagement demonstrated an improvement in their understanding and practice of the teaching of writing in the English curriculum and their understanding and practice of collaborative inquiry as a cornerstone of a professional learning community.

From a research perspective the two years were distinctive and involved the use of different methods of data gathering. Year one was the introductory year of building understanding and 'growing' trust in the belief that 'trust is the first level at getting to a professional learning community' (Hord, 2004: 77). Learning collaborative inquiry through doing collaborative inquiry was underpinned by developing teachers' knowledge, skills and dispositions about teaching writing as the needs were manifested. With the explicit intention of promoting the professionalism of the teachers, the programme included developing participants' understanding of the theory of action that informed the programme (Wiliam and Thompson, 2007). By theory of action I mean developing an understanding of the concept of the school as a professional learning community as the context for empowering professional learning. Data gathering in year one was informed by Guskey's (2002) five-level approach to professional development and included an end of year survey, teacher interviews, minutes of meetings and facilitator's reflective journal.

In year two, as participants' confidence in the process grew, and taking the cue from the findings at the end of year one, the teachers' role became more central and data gathering focused on teachers' peer-to-peer dialogue. This was based on the findings that teachers rated teacher-to-teacher talk as highly significant in shaping professional practice. The nature of that influence was not really understood. The learning gained from this phase of data gathering is the subject of another paper. But suffice it to say that as a result a number of teachers volunteered to have one of their lessons videoed and later shown to their peers in their TPLT meeting. In what became known as teachers' post-observation discussions, the members of the TPLT then shared feedback on the recorded lesson. These shared feedback discussions were video-recorded, analysed using a form of discourse analysis called Systemic Functional Linguistics (SFL). SFL employs analytical tools to examine the intended purposes of words, the reasons why they make the meanings they do and the values that they reveal (Martin and Rose, 2007). The findings were fed back to the teachers to better understand the sometimes conflicting frameworks that underpinned their practice.

Some of the learning gained from this research will be presented in narrative form around two key images that captured the process of this inquiry.

1 Facilitating whole school professional learning involves a multi-level approach

Schools are complex systems (Senge et al., 2000). Facilitating adaptive change that challenges deeply held values and beliefs (Heifetz et al., 2009), recognises the complexity and interrelatedness operating at multi-levels throughout the school. Figure 8.1 captures the framework that was developed to help see through that complexity. It involved working at a number of levels simultaneously in an iterative, cyclical process: organisational level in setting up structures and artefacts to support the intervention; cultural level in exploring the concepts through workshops for full teaching staff; and pedagogical level in focusing on specifics of classroom practice. Using a metaphor from photography, to the degree that work at the level of the teacher learning teams was zooming in on the minutia of classroom practice, so might the work at full teaching staff level, through regular workshops, be considered zooming out to understand the broader cultural panorama.

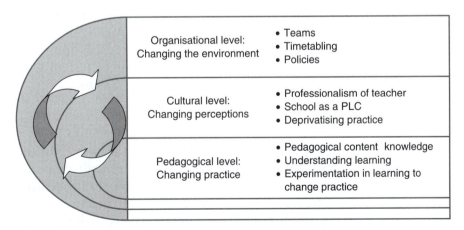

Figure 8.1   Facilitating multi-level school change

Organisational level

Setting up the structures to support the programme was one of the first requirements. Teacher professional learning teams (TPLT), based on reflective professional enquiry and opening up personal practice, were the basic building blocks of the intervention. While teachers had a clear choice to engage or not in the research-oriented activities such as being involved in the data gathering, there was an expectation once the whole teaching staff made the decision to engage with the process that every teacher assign themselves to a learning team. This was deemed a professional expectation. However, simply forming teams is not enough to lead to professional learning. Watkins (2005) recognised that it cannot be assumed that teachers will have the experience and models to do this, it must be learned. It was a key function of the external facilitator to co-create a structure, format and guiding principles for all meetings, otherwise they run the danger of simply involving storytelling and not leading to purposeful action for improvement.

Sharing personal practice involves generally opening up the classroom doors, metaphorically and physically, to deprivatise their daily way of doing things. Learning how to see, and share feedback on, another's practice is highly sensitive and requires professional learning. It involved modelling and practising a feedback-meeting format within a non-threatening, contrived context prior to putting it into practice. The meeting format was inspired by the work of Egan (2001), Carnell et al. (2006), Dennison and Kirk (1990), loosely based on a peer coaching structure to adapt to any focus of learning and inquiry.

Time for meetings was, and remained, a serious challenge throughout the intervention. Although all the directives from DES and the Teaching Council in Ireland strongly recommend collaborative practice in schools, it remains a mystery how collaboration can effectively happen when there is no scheduled time to do so. It is left to school leaders to find 'creative' ways for so doing. This is a highly unprofessional modus operandi, and an avoidance, by those at system level leadership, of tackling the bigger question of time in school.

Cultural level

Initially it was thought that the role of the external facilitator would be to work closely with the team of in-school facilitators (FT) in building their capacity to work with their own peers at the TPLT meetings. Here we met the first hurdle of cultural norms of practice. At an exploratory meeting, teachers felt that their peers would deem it too presumptuous to put themselves forward as in-school facilitators in such a role. Knowing from personal experience the cultural binds that influence our practice, I suggested that at the next staff meeting I would lead a workshop on our professional learning initiative during the course of which I would raise the issue of the role of facilitators. I felt this was a critical point in building trust in, and consensus for, the project. The teachers needed to trust the facilitator to negotiate a way through the cultural norms of practice that would not leave anyone exposed and at the same time raise issues that needed to be tackled. So began the process of the external facilitator's dual level of engagement: to work closely with the in-school facilitators but also at the level of the full teaching staff. The first staff meeting each term was facilitated by me and became the forum for engaging in healthy professional dialogue, asking the big questions and raising what Barth calls the non-discussables in schools (Barth, 2001). This became crucial to the process in changing perceptions and without working at this level I believe the intervention would have remained marginal to real school practice. Developing teacher agency must be at the heart of professional learning and demands that structures are provided for teachers' voices to be heard and acted on. Key learnings from this:

1 Roles created to support the developing PLC must make explicit their leadership dimension to avoid individual incumbents having to negotiate the space to do so.

2 The presence of an experienced external facilitator can create the conditions for school staffs to face the cultural impediments that may reside within their communities and to draw out the fundamental aspiration of the individual teacher, the moral purpose that underpins actions.

Pedagogical level
At their first meeting the facilitators, in discussing the subject matter, voiced their concerns that one cannot teach what one does not know and not all subjects are learned in the same way. In doing so they identified the need to develop what Shulman (1987) calls pedagogical content knowledge. Shulman argued that a combination of content knowledge and pedagogical knowledge – *pedagogical content knowledge* – plays a crucial role in leading school improvement (Entwistle and Smith, 2002). As a result, teachers with expertise were identified and invited to share that expertise. External expertise was also brought in by inviting guest speakers as needed. It was decided to adopt the genre-based approach to teaching writing (Kress, 1994). From then on through the meetings needs were

identified and the school leadership worked with the teachers in finding ways of responding to those needs: a workshop led by an external expert was organised on Assessment for Learning; the school intranet was developed to share resources; a notice board in the staff room was dedicated to genre writing and was updated regularly throughout the research; website resources were shared and used; teachers developed their own assessment rubrics. Each meeting gave as much time to 'how' as to 'what' of teaching writing, keeping in mind the advice from Joyce and Showers that 'the content needs to elevate what is taught, how it is taught and the social climate of the school. A good innovation that simply replaces a good practice is unlikely to increase student learning capacity' (Joyce and Showers, 2002: 5).

2 Learning collaborative practice requires supporting teacher agency and differentiation

Facilitating in-school collaborative learning for professional practice in an Irish primary school involved major cultural change given teachers' 'legendary autonomy' (OECD, 1991). During the course of a workshop led by Professor John West-Burnham at the end of phase one, the teachers identified the greatest cultural change of this intervention as moving from a view of teaching as private and personal to one of teaching as public and collaborative, nurturing experimentation and sharing.

Making explicit their understanding of collaborative practice, the teachers originally identified six levels (see Figure 8.2) on that journey from level one, sharing planning, at the top to level six, sharing improvements, at the deepest level. By the end of the intervention this had become seven levels. The model suggests that level one, sharing planning, is only the tip of the iceberg when it comes to learning collaborative practice but a good place to start in that most Irish teachers are now comfortable at that level of collaboration. As teachers progress downwards, they go deeper into understanding their own practice and learning, and the effects become more widely felt through the school the deeper they go. Significantly, they envisioned the process leading to sharing observation, feedback and improvement and that this was a realistic target. Thus the goal was clearly stated and the road to getting there was mapped out by the teachers who would be taking the journey. In the light of the evidence available that goal was a given but the means of getting there allowed for difference in pacing. Every teacher could identify where they were on that learning journey and as they were ready to move on they could do so. That initiative had to come from them but the influence of one or two positive voices powerfully

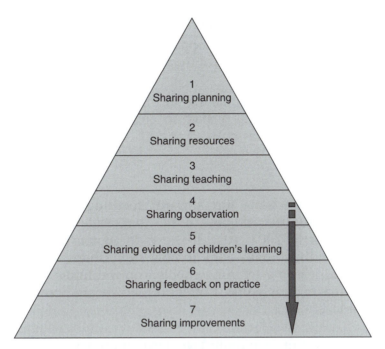

Figure 8.2 Conceptual model for learning collaborative practice

impacted on the success of the intervention. At the end of the intervention there were people at all levels of the scale but some had shared observation and most had engaged in learning how to give feedback. They had also shared evidence of improvement. This was achieved through getting hard data on each pupil's pre-teaching and post-teaching standard of writing in the case of a particular genre and making that data public. The data categorically showed an improvement across all classes in terms of the standard of writing. The criteria for assessment were rubric-based and drawn up by the teachers. To ensure objectivity the grading of the work was done by one non-mainstream class teacher.

That the teachers were actively involved in creating the scaffolding for their own learning to engage in collaborative practice and inquiry was highly influential in the process. Furthermore, it greatly reduced the fears that teachers had expressed about the process as their own agency was supported. The progression from one stage to another involved prior learning of the processes and procedures that are needed to professionally engage at each level. Teachers saw the idea of collaborative inquiry as something that has to be learned, as involving the creation of new norms of practice, as potentially confidence-building and incremental. This visual imaging of the concept helped to:

- clarify where the process was leading – map the journey;
- make visible the inherent opportunity for teachers to make a professional choice to move from one level to the next as they were ready to do so;
- facilitate the teachers making an informed choice when committing themselves as a staff to engage in the collaborative inquiry process.

The postlude

This research goes some way towards focusing on 'the teacher learning opportunities and possibilities that reside within ordinary daily work' (Little, 2003: 104). It shows the potential that resides within that ordinary daily work to powerfully shape the quality of teaching and learning in Irish schools into the future. To support schools in making this happen I offer the following recommendations at system level.

1 At the heart of such multi-level facilitation lies an unwavering commitment to dialogic action and inquiry (Habermas, 1998; Yankelovich, 2001). By dialogic action I mean a commitment to ongoing egalitarian discussion and critical inquiry resulting in participative negotiation of the theory of action itself and of all actions to be taken. The facilitator, in my view, keeps multiple conversations alive and in dialogue throughout the process, even when that means simply holding them on 'pause'. This requires qualified facilitation by facilitators who understand professionally respectful and agency-building learning and can hold that in balance with the professional obligation to continually challenge and raise quality of service. I suggest that access to such qualified facilitation should be made available to all schools. Such qualification should include the learning of expertise in coaching and mentoring for professional learning in education. I see this as keeping learning on track through an independent voice continuing to ask the hard questions and thus avoiding the danger of complacency. I believe this is where the university–schools link, emphasised in Chapter 7, would be mutually enriching.

2 The question of time in school must be resolved. The need for schools to develop as professional learning communities is no longer an option. In order to do so, teachers must have the time to meet and collaborate in a formalised manner.

3   The expectation that all teachers engage in meaningful professional learning should be made mandatory through the Teaching Council. The current situation, where the school is statutorily bound to provide professional learning with no corresponding obligation on the part of teachers, is untenable. How that should be done would have to be seriously considered in light of the educatively negative associations with externally imposed mandates.

4   Teacher professional learning should incorporate the knowledge, skills, dispositions and intellectual stimulation to lead to ongoing learning throughout their careers. It must include deep understanding around learning and how people learn. In addition the skills for today's teachers must include learning how to gather and process appropriate data to inform a more evidence-based practice. It would seem that to date much of our professional development practice talks about developing constructivist practices in our classrooms while walking the walk of the transmission model of learning.

5   I believe there is vagueness around the concept of teacher professionalism in Ireland. I suggest that the lack of an informed membership in this regard leaves both the profession as a whole, and the teachers as individuals, the poorer for it. I suggest that this is something to which the Teaching Council might give consideration.

6   Finally, it has long being claimed that teachers hold a vice-like grip on their autonomy and that the privacy of their practice is a deeply held value (Johnson and Donaldson, 2007; Little, 1990). The findings from this research suggest that in fact, when professionally negotiated in a process that respects their professionalism through building their capacity to exercise agency, teachers place collaborative practice above privacy. I also suggest that it is individual and collective agency that is valued by teachers rather than the proverbial autonomy (Lortie, 1975).

Finally, it is time that the paralysis that seems to pervade our system is tackled. Why is it that:

> One of the great paradoxes of modern Irish education is that, while the official discourse is replete with references to change and reform, much of the available evidence suggests that little change has occurred in teachers' beliefs and values. (Gleeson and O'Donnabháin, 2009: 37)

References

Barber, M. and Mourshed, M. (2007) *How the World's Best-Performing School Systems Come out on Top*. London: McKinsey and Company.

Barth, R.S. (2001) *Learning by Heart*. San Francisco: Jossey-Bass.

Burnette, B. (2002) 'How we formed our community', *Journal of Staff Development*, 23(1).

Carnell, E., MacDonald, J. and Askew, S. (2006) *Coaching and Mentoring in Higher Education*. London: Institute of Education, University of London.

Coolahan, J. (2007) *A Review Paper on Thinking and Policies Relating to Teacher Education in Ireland: Paper prepared by Professor John Coolahan for the Teaching Council*. Maynooth: The Teaching Council.

Dennison, B. and Kirk, R. (1990) *Do, Review, Learn and Apply: A Simple Guide to Experiential Learning*. Oxford: Blackwell.

Egan, G. (2001) *The Skilled Helper: A Problem Management and Opportunity-Development Approach to Helping*. London: Wadsworth.

Entwistle, N. and Smith, C. (2002) 'Personal understanding and target understanding: mapping influences on the outcomes of learning', *British Journal of Educational Psychology*, 72(3): 321–42.

Gleeson, J. and O'Donnabháin, D. (2009) 'Strategic planning and accountability in Irish education', *Irish Educational Studies*, 28(1): 27–46.

Grossman, P., Wineburg, S. and Woolworth, S. (2000) 'What makes teacher community different from a gathering of teachers?', available online. Full-Text Availability Options: PDF ERIC Full Text (1439k) … last accessed 22 July 2007.

Guskey, T.R. (2000) *Evaluating Professional Development*. Thousand Oaks, CA: Corwin Press.

Guskey, T.R. (2002) 'Professional development and teacher change', *Teachers and Teaching: Theory and Practice*, 8(3): 381–91.

Habermas, J. (1998) *The Inclusion of the Other: Studies in Political Theory*. Cambridge, MA: MIT Press.

Heifetz, R., Grashow, A. and Linsky, M. (2009) *The Practice of Adaptive Leadership*. Harvard: Harvard Business Press.

Hord, S.M. (2004) *Learning Together, Leading Together: Changing Schools Through Professional Learning Communities*. Austin, Texas: SEDL.

Johnson, S.M. and Donaldson, M.L. (2007) 'Overcoming obstacles to leadership', *Educational Leadership*, 65(1): 8–13.

Joyce, B. and Showers, B. (2002) *Student Achievement Through Staff Development* (3rd edn). Alexandria, VA: ASCD.

Konstantopoulos, S. (2006) 'Trends of school effects on student achievement: evidence from NLS: 72 and NELS: 92'. *Teachers College Record*, 108(12): 2550–81. Available at: www.tcrecord.org.

Kress, G. (1994) *Learning to Write* (2nd edn). London: Routledge.

Little, J.W. (1990) 'The persistence of privacy: autonomy and initiative in teachers' professional relations', *Teachers College Record*, 91(4): 509–36.

Little, J.W. (2003) 'Inside teacher community: representations of classroom practice', *Teachers College Record*, 105(6): 913–45, available online at http://www. torecord.org/content.asp: contentid=11544, last accessed 5 April 2008.

Lortie, D.C. (1975) *Schoolteacher: A Sociological Study*. Chicago, IL: University of Chicago Press.

Louis, K.S. (2006) *Organizing for School Change: Contexts of Learning*. Abingdon, Oxon: Routledge.

Loxley, A., Johnston, K., Murchan, D., Fitzgerald, H. and Quinn, M. (2007) 'The role of whole school contexts in shaping the experiences and outcomes associated with professional development', *Professional Development in Education*, 33(3): 265–85.

MacBeath, J., Gray, J., Cullen, J., Frost, D., Steward, S. and Swaffield, S. (2007) *Schools On The Edge Responding to Challenging Circumstances*. London: Paul Chapman Publishing.

McLaughlin, M. and Talbert, J.E. (2006) *Building School-Based Teacher Learning Communities: Professional Strategies to Improve Student Achievement*. New York: Teachers College Press.

Martin, J.R. and Rose, D. (2007) *Working with Discourse: Meaning beyond the Clause* (2nd edn). London: Continuum.

NCCA (2008) *Primary Curriculum Review, Phase 2: Final Report with Recommendations*. Dublin: NCCA, available on-line at www.ncca.ie/publicationslreports

OECD (1991) *Reviews of National Education Policies for Education: Ireland*. Paris: OECD.

Senge, P., Cambron-McCabe, N., Lucas, T., Smith, B., Dutton, J. and Kleiner, A. (2000) *Schools that Learn: A Fifth Handbook for Educators, Parents and Everyone Who Cares about Education*. New York: Doubleday.

Stoll, L., Bolam, R., McMahon, A., Thomas, S., Wallace, M., Greenwood, A. and Hawkey. K. (2006) *Professional Learning Communities: Source Materials for School Leaders and Other Leaders of Professional Learning*. Nottingham: National College of School Leadership.

Shulman, L. (1987) 'Knowledge and teaching: foundations of the new reform', *Harvard Educational Review*, 57(1): 1–22.

Sugrue, C. (2002) 'Irish teachers' experiences of professional learning: implications for policy and practice', *Professional Development in Education*, 28(2): 311–38.

Watkins, C. (2005) *Classrooms as Learning Communities: What's in it for Schools?* Abingdon, Oxon: Routledge.

Wiliam, D. and Thompson, M. (2007) 'Tight but loose: a conceptual framework for scaling up school reforms', Annual Meeting of the American Educational Research Association (AERA). Chicago, IL.

Yankelovich, D. (2001) *The Magic of Dialogue: Transforming Conflict into Cooperation*. New York: Touchstone, Simon and Schuster.

Chapter 9

School Leadership for Special Educational Needs

Michael Shevlin and Paula Flynn

Abstract

Responding appropriately to the varied requirements of children with special educational needs within schools is a complex, challenging task. Informed, capable school leadership is an essential prerequisite for the development of a suitable learning environment for children and young people who have been identified as experiencing special educational needs. However, within an Irish context there is little evidence that the connection between school leadership and effective provision for children and young people who have special educational needs has been extensively explored. Inclusive schools emphasise the presence, participation and achievement of children with special educational needs in all aspects of school life. Developing inclusive learning environments is a continuous process that involves building the capacity of school leaders and staff to respond appropriately to the needs of all learners within the school community. School leadership in the area of special educational needs is a challenging task that requires a leader who is able to articulate a vision for inclusive education and can motivate staff to collaborate in the establishment of inclusive school cultures. When asked to encapsulate the role of principal with regards to 'leadership and special educational needs', Sarah, our case study principal, says, 'The role of the principal is pivotal; the leader of the school has to have courage to act.'

Key words

Inclusive learning environments; special educational needs; school community; participation; school leadership.

Introduction

Responding appropriately to the varied requirements of children with special educational needs within schools is a complex, challenging task. Informed, capable school leadership is an essential prerequisite for the development of a suitable learning environment for children and young people who have been identified as experiencing special educational needs. However, within an Irish context there is little evidence that the connection between school leadership and effective provision for children and young people who have special educational needs has been extensively explored. Within this chapter we will examine developments in understanding special educational needs and the implications for school leadership. We will also present an in-depth case study of one school leader and document the critical issues faced in conceptualising and implementing a more inclusive approach towards children and young people experiencing special educational needs.

International developments

Government policies internationally have established the rights of students with disabilities and/or special educational needs (SEN) to be educated in mainstream schools. The Salamanca statement (UNESCO, 1994), for example, declared that schools should accommodate all children including those with a disability and/or special educational need. The Salamanca statement has had a profound impact on thinking and policy formulation in the area of inclusive education. It is argued very cogently within the statement that mainstream schools with an inclusive orientation are:

> the most effective means of combating discriminatory attitudes, building an inclusive society and achieving education for all. (UNESCO, 1994: ix)

More recently, the Dakar statement (UNESCO, 2000) emanating from a World Education Forum, affirmed an international commitment to education for all children in inclusive, educational environments.

The adoption of the United Nations Convention on the Rights of Persons with Disabilities (2006) marked a significant landmark in international developments in recognising the urgency of addressing the needs of this marginalised population. To date 86 countries have fully ratified the convention, though Ireland has failed to do so. Ratifying this convention imposes on signatory states the submission of regular reports on its progress and implementation.

Specific legislation has supported the right of students with disabilities and/or special educational needs to be educated in mainstream schools, particularly in the USA, United Kingdom, Canada and Australia, that aim to reflect diversity. Diversity in the mainstream is gaining acceptance worldwide. The current tendency in Europe is towards developing a policy of inclusion. For example, the European Agency for Development in Special Needs Education (2009) has published an extensive set of indicators of inclusive education based on consultation with EU member states.

Despite the emphasis on inclusion and inclusive practice within policy and legislation internationally a fully accepted definition of inclusion has yet to emerge. Thomas and O' Hanlon (2004) emphasise an education system that values diversity and equity rather than simply concentrating on those children and young people who have special educational needs. Educational inclusion involves a fundamental restructuring of the education system to facilitate all children to participate and achieve within mainstream settings:

> … educational inclusion, which we see in terms of the presence, participation and achievement of all students in local mainstream schools, rather than simply focusing on any one group of vulnerable learners. This means that we see the task of inclusion as being essentially transformative, requiring better use of available resources to improve policies and practices. It also leads us to argue that existing arrangements, at all levels of the education system create barriers for learners. (Ainscow et al., 2003: 230)

Policy and legislation within the Republic of Ireland

Within the past two decades Ireland has witnessed the development of public policy and legislation that attempts to enshrine the rights of the child to an appropriate education. Within this broad policy thrust there has been an emergence of a sustained commitment to ensure equitable access to resources for disadvantaged communities including children with disabilities and/or special educational needs. Equality and access through legislation and the mainstreaming of services has become a cornerstone of government policy. Within education this has resulted in special educational provision being increasingly located in mainstream schools.

Irish education experienced a dearth of legislation (Ministerial/ DES circulars regulating provision were prevalent) until the 1998 Education Act. Crucially, the Act stipulated equality and parental choice which, according to Meaney et al. (2005) constituted a first step towards inclusive education. The Education for Persons with Special Educational Needs (EPSEN) Act of 2004 marked a significant milestone in Irish educational legislation. A central objective of the Act was to establish the provision of inclusive learning environments and ensure that children and young people with special educational needs were afforded the opportunity to benefit from education, participate within society and lead independent lives. School principals are expected to assume a significant degree of responsibility for establishing a coherent system of special educational provision and ensuring that the child's current special educational needs are effectively addressed. This involves the development of school SEN policy, setting up effective identification and assessment procedures, establishing a support infrastructure, ensuring curricular access and liaising with a variety of government agencies. While some of these duties can be devolved to a special educational needs coordinator and/or SEN team the ultimate responsibility and accountability remains with the school principal.

School leadership and special educational needs

School leadership generally consists of providing direction and exercising influence (Leithwood and Riehl, 2003). School leaders provide direction for the school community through the creation of a shared purpose and vision for the education of children and young people. Exercising influence in the school community involves the school leader 'galvanizing effort around ambitious goals and create conditions that support teachers and help students succeed' (Leithwood and Riehl, 2003: 2). In particular, school leaders will identify and articulate a vision, create shared meaning and strengthen school culture through the development of collaborative practices and processes.

Developing inclusive learning environments requires a significant modification of how schooling and learning have traditionally been conceptualised. Ainscow et al. (2006) characterise inclusive schools as those which attempt to: (a) focus on all children and young people in the school; (b) emphasise presence, participation and achievement in all aspects of school life; and (c) view the development of inclusive learning environments as a continuous process. This process involves building the capacity of school leaders and staff to respond appropriately to the needs of all learners within the school community (Devecchi and Nevin, 2010). Ainsow et al. (2006) and Ainscow and Sandhill (2010) argue very persuasively that the critical factor in developing inclusive learning environments requires an understanding of the social processes in a given context and the thinking that informs these processes and subsequent practice:

> the development of more inclusive approaches does not arise from a mechanical process in which any one specific organisational restructuring, or the introduction of a particular set of techniques, generates increased levels of participation. Rather, as we have argued, the development of inclusive practices requires processes of social learning within particular organisational contexts. (Ainscow and Sandhill, 2010: 404)

School culture

School culture is a critical determinant of the inclusive nature of a school and the principal is a central figure in the development of a culture that welcomes diversity and is proactive in addressing the individual and varied needs of children and young people (Hattie, 2005). Within a small-scale study recently conducted in the Republic of Ireland (Shevlin et al., 2009) there is ample evidence that school principals are actively engaged in the development of inclusive learning environments.

Inclusive practice was reported by a principal in a large urban school to improve the general atmosphere in the school as there was increased respect between school leaders, teachers and pupils:

> I'd be really proud of the atmosphere in the school – the way in general that students treat teachers and teachers treat students. There's a real element of respect around the school I think and it's often been noted you know when people come in … from other schools. (Principal, 457, original transcript)

Well, I think there's great communication between the staff and management, I think it is very inclusive, there's a great emphasis on academic but also on extra-curricular and there's a huge weight of extra-curricular activities that take place within the school and people are very positive about the school. I think students find it better to see a productive environment in which to come to school in, I think that's very important. (Classroom teacher, 478, original transcript)

School enrolment policy can be a critical indicator of school thinking with regards to the inclusion of children and young people with special educational needs. One principal (Shevlin et al., 2009) conceptualised an inclusive school as embracing a wider range of pupils than those with special educational needs:

When I look in an inclusive school I am thinking of our international pupils and our traveller pupils so I'm thinking of encompassing the whole lot – that you have open access for all pupils coming into your school so that your enrolment policy is the starting point, they know from your enrolment policy that all children are welcome into your school. Then that there is no exclusion clause really and hopefully that you are able to provide a differentiated teaching programme within your school ... (Principal, 445, original transcript)

The following principal was very aware of the need to be flexible in developing an inclusion policy and ensuring that the school community was fully involved:

We're at the process of drafting one, I suppose it's an issue that we've discussed over the past two or three years and we're very conscious as a staff of creating, I suppose, I couldn't say policy but creating guidelines and procedures that would help especially new teachers and for new staff on where we're at and where we're going. I suppose the key to any good policy is to know where you're coming from and where you're going to and I suppose we're adapting and developing. (Principal, 276, original transcript)

Appropriateness of inclusion

School principals play a critical role in determining the appropriateness of inclusion for pupils who experience particular forms of special educational needs. Avramidis and Norwich (2002) reported that doubts about the appropriateness of inclusion for some children appear to depend on the type and severity of disability and/or special educational need. School principals in Shevlin et al.'s (2009) study while positive about the inherent value of inclusion, discussed fears about including children with significant needs they had not experienced before as explained by one principal in a small town:

> I suppose we haven't had to date applications from … we haven't had any autistic children but I suppose I would have had worries about anxieties if we had an application for a severely autistic child or severe behavioural difficulties, I would look on what we have had as very mild … (Principal, 447, original transcript)

Where principals had direct experience some concerns were evident in relation to children with moderate learning difficulties:

> And I would think of that pupil who had a moderate learning difficulty…. even with the support of a special needs assistant, I suppose she was integrated as socially as she could be, yet I think that the guilt here would be more with the class teacher, feeling that she wasn't able to do enough for her. (Principal, 448, original transcript)

Accommodating and effectively including children who have significantly challenging behaviour were reported to be concerns in mainstream schools (Cole, 2005). Teacher stress, frustration and low self esteem are reported to be frequent costs of such efforts. The participants in Shevlin et al.'s (2009) study perceived that social, emotional and behavioural difficulties were increasing in terms of severity, complexity and prevalence:

> … behavioural difficulties, the destructive nature in the classroom gives the class teacher huge challenges and it is that you are so long waiting for the resources to be put in place – the only thing really that excludes students from anything in our school is behaviour. (Principal, 447, original transcript)

Fostering inclusion

Fostering inclusive practice in schools is associated with a proactive leadership style rather than a reactive management style (Horne and

Timmons, 2009). Winter and Kilpatrick (2001) in a cross-jurisdictional study comparing findings between schools in Ontario and schools in Northern Ireland reported that the role of the principal was critical in the internal support system within the school. Principals' support and direct participation were seen as key factors in the success of inclusive practice and this role extended beyond allocation of resources and included collaborative efforts to promote inclusion. Whole school approaches are essential and inclusion cannot be the sole responsibility of the principal and/or SEN support team, as articulated by one principal in Shevlin et al.'s (2009) study:

> Well, I think the openness and willingness of the staff, that they're welcoming, and I think the pupils themselves are very welcoming of new children but also as they go up through the school that they are so supportive of children that have special needs, especially when they come to fifth and sixth class. If you have some low incidence pupils then there may be issues around their social interaction and that and the other pupils are just so accommodating of those children. (Principal, 216, original transcript)

Participants in the above study concluded that inclusion required a focus on leadership, management, organisation of curriculum, teaching methodologies, learning styles, and the physical layout of the school. One principal developed this further by proposing that the creation of an inclusive learning environment involved a particular inclusive thinking style on the part of all school staff, which originates from the top in terms of leadership. The conditions conducive to effective inclusion include strong relationships, open, honest communication, open-mindedness, and a positive, unthreatening, welcoming atmosphere in the school environment, a view corroborated in the research literature (Horne and Timmons, 2009; Loreman, 2000). Successful inclusion in a challenging situation appears to provide schools with the confidence and skills required for further developing inclusive practice.

Within the following case study the leadership role as experienced by a principal in an urban-based, co-educational, post-primary school has been documented.

Case study: Sarah Jenkins

Background and influences
Sarah Jenkins identifies a culmination of influences and experiences as highly significant within her style of leadership. Having a sibling

with dyslexia meant that from an early age she understood that children have very different experiences of school, depending on their access to learning and the capacity of a school to meet the needs of its students. Within her first teaching post, Sarah had the opportunity to work closely with and learn from the learning support teacher in that school. She attributes this opportunity as the most influential experience of her life. The school in which she was teaching had in place a policy of inclusion, and the learning support teacher was involved in every aspect of school life, supporting both teachers and students in pursuit of strategies to meet the needs of children with learning difficulties. Sarah was very impressed with the model of provision within that school and the commitment to 'learning for all students'. The fundamental objectives of this model are what she has subscribed to throughout her career both as a learning support teacher and currently as a principal.

Prior to her current post in St Christopher's College, Sarah was a special educational needs coordinator (SENCO) in a school where the principal was both visionary and highly supportive. He provided opportunities, which she availed of, to expand both her role and the department within the school. Initially there was resentment amongst a small number of staff, some of whom were dismayed that Sarah's success with students was encouraging the 'wrong type' of students to the school. She pursued and completed the Higher Diploma in Remedial Teaching, within which there was a strong emphasis on the role of the special needs teacher relative to the organisation and leadership of the school. As SENCO in her last post, Sarah was involved in every aspect of school life, which she believes both influenced and informed her for the role of principal.

Taking on a leadership role

The school in which Sarah became principal already had a solid reputation for looking after children with special educational needs. However, the perception of the school was that it accommodated children who did not have great ambition academically and a lot of students, particularly those with special needs, traditionally did not stay beyond the legal school-leaving age. Sarah identifies the model of special needs provision as one of 'sympathy' rather than 'empowerment and learning'. One of her immediate impressions and concerns was that a lot of the children seemed to have a very negative 'identity', perceiving themselves to be within a school to which students came if they could not get into a better school. She describes the atmosphere as 'charged' among the children, especially in the yard, with examples of very 'bad' and antisocial behaviour. However, she quickly discovered that the perpetrators of this behaviour were completely different when she spoke to them on a one-to-one basis, which seemed to indicate a difficulty situated in the dynamic of the school rather than attributed to the children individually.

Sarah immediately set out to identify what constructive changes would have the most benefits and far-reaching consequences for all the children in the school. Focusing on issues such as fostering a 'positive identity' for the individual student as well as for the entire student body, she decided to tackle the ability grouping model that had existed until her appointment. The school was streamed and there were few choices available to children once they were categorised as within a specific range of ability. It was clear to her that from day one, children were put into a stream in which they stayed and opportunities were not available for children in lower streams, who subsequently were not being challenged. Difficult and challenging behaviour was highly prevalent in lower streams and unfortunately a culture of acceptance of this had become the practice. Sarah described the experience of the children in lower streams as sustaining a 'self-fulfilling prophesy' of underachievement, despite the anomaly that it was set within a very caring environment.

The major changes she set out to achieve were: moving from streaming to mixed ability, a collaborative model of taking responsibility amongst staff and dissemination of information. Within the Special Needs Department there had been a lot of control and protection of information, leading to reluctance in sharing details of the needs of children with assessments. Sarah gradually facilitated a change towards a more systemic approach to provision of special needs which was closer to the system she had previously worked within, which included the organisation and structure of SNAs with the appointment of one SNA as coordinator.

Motivation, collaboration and teamwork

Sarah stresses the importance of being able to motivate members of staff to become participants and drivers of change. The ability to do this is dependent on the response from individuals but also on a certain amount of instinct on the part of the principal as leader. Sarah closely examined the system that had been in place prior to her appointment. She identified areas which needed the input of staff members in teams that would facilitate a smooth and participatory transition to update existing structures or introduce new provisions or services. The Second Level Support Services (SLSS) had been very helpful in guiding the staff on formulating and organising a school plan. However, within the school there was a tradition of committee meetings during school time. Sarah believed that given the number of systemic changes she wished to introduce, such as the move from streaming to mixed ability, it was important to develop a culture of team meetings outside school time. She organised early morning breakfast meetings at which she provided breakfast to encourage involvement and attendance. She also organised after school team meetings in venues outside the school, sometimes with a social aspect, for year heads and other groups. Initially these meetings were met with a lot of opposition but in time it was seen that when meetings took place outside school hours, they were organised in such a manner as to acknowledge the good work that was being done, encouraging and reinforcing collegiality.

Overall, Sarah believes the process was highly productive and the alliance of opposition was broken. This was largely due to the positive attitude of staff, who felt they were valued and acknowledged, but most of all because it was clear that Sarah, as principal, was adamant about the need for progression in this manner and was intent on showing leadership. Some of the teams, committees and groups who worked collaboratively were: year heads, the Care Team, the Post Review Committee, the Critical Incident Policy Group, Drug Response Group and the Mixed Ability Review Group. Despite the fact that there was some resistance initially both to the change to 'mixed ability' and the collaboration of the teams in general, there was acknowledgement that the previous system wasn't working. Sarah admitted that she chose to ignore the opposition and made involvement on all teams completely voluntary, but ultimately changes were made because of her insistence as principal. She points out that when she arrived at the school, 'everything was working but nothing was connected'.

Vision for special educational needs

Sarah explains that her vision for the provision of special educational needs is that there should be no difference between children in a school but instead a model should exist where education is provided for *all the children who are there*, meeting their requirements. Apart from designated special educational needs, children experience other difficulties arising from issues such as emotional difficulties, poverty and general disadvantage. It is important, Sarah stresses, to have structures to support children in whatever way they need that support. She points out that if you do what is needed, it is probably the right thing; you need to find out from a student what they need, rather than telling them what they need. Her vision within the school is of having a system in place to respond in this way to every child. In order to achieve this, she explains 'you need the school to be highly organised, people need to be very flexible, you need to create a "can do" atmosphere and a place where it is accepted that people are allowed to make mistakes ... it is highly liberating.' Once children are learning in an atmosphere that encourages effort and does not criticise mistakes, they are empowered to participate within school and can do so with more confidence and less fear of rejection.

In Sarah's experience encouraging teachers to accept new methods or ways of doing things can be challenging, which is why it is helpful to avail of influences from outside the school in order to convince staff of the benefits. With this also, you need strong leadership and colleagues who are prepared to work together. She explains that

> when you are doing your job by supporting people – you are also saying to them, quite obviously I can't do any more than I am doing now ... so take some responsibility yourself ... because sometimes it is too easy to hand over a problem to other people.

Sarah believes it is fundamental that 'learning support', 'resource provision' and 'school guidance' feed into and inform the role of the year head, working within a structured system of collaboration. Sharing information contributes significantly in the implementation of successful strategies to support students and/or prevent challenging behaviour. Until recently, a lot of the children with special needs in the school were not registering for further education. However, new initiatives on the part of the School Guidance Counsellor, supported within this systemic approach, have resulted in a significant increase in the numbers applying for third level courses.

Despite the fact that a caring environment had always existed at St Christopher's College, 'sometimes it was almost too much so', according to Sarah. It can be disempowering for children with SEN if they are cared for without expectations or attention to learning, thus fostering 'helplessness'. It is crucial, in Sarah's opinion, that there is a strong focus on 'learning' and providing the best opportunities to do so for every student. This can be achieved by examining all the data provided from assessments, reports and results, meeting needs appropriately and cultivating a more positive approach among students and teachers. It is imperative not to accept the attitude that a student is 'stuck with a difficulty'. Throughout her career, Sarah's main focus and concern has always been about finding out 'how a student learns'. She is concerned that a fundamental disrespect for children and particularly for anybody with any kind of difficulties exists among some people and asserts that 'we think we do something for the children ... but really there is a sense that if somebody has difficulties that in fact they *are* the difficulty rather than the "system" might be *wrong*.'

Inclusion

Sarah is adamant that if we are to achieve full implementation of 'Inclusion' as a policy within Irish education, firstly this must be a feature of *all* schools and secondly, it only exists when all human life is represented in the school. She emphasises that a school should have among its student population a true representation of the families and children in the local area:

> There is a great necessity for strong policy from government on this because it is essential that all schools are inclusive, there is a limit to the balance that can be sustained if the expectation is only on certain schools to provide for children with special needs. It is fundamental to the successful implementation of the policy that all schools should provide appropriate education and meet the additional needs where necessary of the children from their catchment area ...

Sarah believes that inclusion is about strengths and acknowledging what people *can* do. Working in teams is the most productive way to promote inclusion as no single person or school has all the answers or can do everything on their own.

Conclusion

School leadership in the area of special educational needs is a challenging task that requires a leader who is able to articulate a vision for inclusive education and can motivate staff to collaborate in the establishment of inclusive school cultures. Believing that all children in the community belong to their local school is an essential first step that needs to be developed into an inclusive style of thinking by all school personnel that ensures that the school is there for all children. When asked to encapsulate the role of principal with regards to 'leadership and special educational needs', Sarah, our case study principal, says, 'The role of the principal is pivotal; the leader of the school has to have courage to act.'

References

Ainscow, M., Booth, T. and Dyson, A. (2006) *Improving Schools, Developing Inclusion*. London: Routledge.

Ainscow, M., Howes, A., Farrell, P. and Frankham, J. (2003) 'Making sense of the development of inclusive practices', *European Journal of Special Needs Education*, 18(2): 227–42.

Ainscow, M. and Sandhill, A. (2010) 'Developing inclusive education systems: The role of organisational cultures and leadership', *International Journal of Inclusive Education*, 14(4): 401–16.

Avramidis, E. and Norwich, B. (2002) 'Mainstream teachers' attitudes towards inclusion/integration: a review of the literature', *European Journal of Special Needs Education*, 17(2): 1–19.

Cole, T. (2005) 'Emotional and behavioural difficulties: an historical perspective', in P. Clough, P. Garner, F. Yuen and J.T. Pardeck (eds), *Handbook of Emotional and Behavioural Difficulties*. London: Sage Publications, pp. 31–44.

Devecchi, C. and Nevin, A. (2010) (in press) 'Leadership in inclusive education', in A. Normore (ed.), *The Development, Preparation, and Socialization of Leaders of Learning-Learners of Leadership: A Global Perspective*. Emerald Series, 'Advances in Educational Administration'.

European Agency for Development in Special Needs Education (2009) Development of a set of indicators for inclusive education in Europe. Brussels: European Agency for Development in Special Needs Education.

Farrell, P. (2004) 'School psychologists: making inclusion a reality for all', *School Psychology International*, 25(1): 5–19.

Government of Ireland (1998) Education Act. Dublin: Stationery Office.

Government of Ireland (2004) Education for Persons with Special Educational Needs Act. Dublin: Stationery Office.

Hattie, J. (2005) 'What is the nature of evidence that makes a difference to learning?', *Special Education Perspectives*, 12: 65–70.

Horne, P. and Timmons, V. (2009) 'Making it work: teachers' perspectives on inclusion', *International Journal of Inclusive Education*, 13(3): 273–86.

Leithwood, K.A. and Riehl, C.J. (2003) *What Do We Already Know about Successful School Leadership?* AERA Division: A Task Force on Developing Research in Educational Leadership. Chicago, IL: AERA.

Loreman, T. (2000) 'School inclusion in Victoria, Australia: the results of six case studies'. Proceedings of the ISEC International Conference 2000.

Meaney, M., Kiernan, N. and Monaohan, K. (2005) *Special Educational Needs and the Law*. Dublin: Thomson Round Hall.

Shevlin, M., Kearns, H., Ranaghan, M., Twomey, M., Smith, R. and Winter, E. (2009) 'Creating inclusive learning environments in Irish schools'. Unpublished report funded by the National Council for Special Education.

Thomas, G. and O' Hanlon, C. (2004) Series editors' preface in G. Thomas and M. Vaughan (eds), *Inclusive Education: Readings and Reflections*. Maidenhead, Berkshire: Open University Press.

UNESCO (2000) Dakar Framework for Action – Education for all, meeting our collective commitment, available at: http://www2.unesco.org/wef/enconf/dakframeng.shtm

United Nations (2006) Draft Convention on the Rights of Persons with Disabilities.

United Nations Educational, Scientific and Cultural Organisation (UNESCO) (1994) The Salamanca statement on principles, policy and practice in special needs education. Paris: UNESCO.

Winter, E.C. and Kilpatrick, R. (2001) 'Special needs resource roles: a cross jurisdictional comparison', *Instructional Psychology*, 28(1): 61–7.

Chapter 10

New Schools for a New Century

Enda McGorman and Martin Wallace

Abstract

This chapter is a reflection by two school principals on their experiences at the time of setting up two new schools, one primary and one post-primary, each on a 'greenfield' site.

In the first section, a primary school principal reflects on the consequences of poor infrastructural planning and educational provision on the early years of the school's development. It captures the experiences and struggles which the school faced as it sought to establish itself as an inclusive school in an increasingly diverse community.

In the second section, the principal reflects on his experiences and thinking at the time of establishing a new greenfield post-primary school. It places an emphasis on building a school community based on dialogue and participation. Partnership with parents, delegation, open communications, developing a mission are among the issues mentioned.

Key words/phrases

Instructional; values; communications; mission; empowerment; school enrolment policy; Section 29 appeals; infrastructural planning; intercultural education; school patronage; ethnic diversity in Ireland; inclusion.

Edna McGorman

A troubled cradling

Mary, Mother of Hope National School was established in 2001 and is situated on the Dublin/Meath border, between Blanchardstown and Clonee. This area has seen massive housing development within the past ten years and, during the boom years of the Celtic Tiger, there seemed to be an inexhaustible demand for housing. Farmland was re-zoned, and estate after estate developed, and occupied. However, in the haste to meet the demands of developer-driven house building, the local authority utterly failed to plan for the educational infrastructure of the area. The implications of this were felt very quickly by our school.

This inability to plan by the local authority was equally evident in the Department of Education and Science (DES). Officials in the Planning Section of the DES had no focused policy or procedures for dealing with the rapidly developing areas which were springing up all over the country and the rigidity and inflexibility of their internal structures left them very poorly equipped to deal with the needs of these areas. As a result, our campus started life in the dreaded prefabricated accommodation and, year on year, the number of prefabs kept on growing. And, as the policymakers struggled to deal with the demands we placed on them, we struggled to deal with the consequences. After our second year of operation, we began to see more and more queries from concerned parents seeking school places for their children. Such was the demand that on our enrolment evening, the queue for places stretched along the prefab corridor, down the hall, round the footpath and onto the main road. The result of this was that the school was, quite literally, overwhelmed by applications for places into Junior Infant class. This presented our Board of Management with an issue which would dominate the agenda for many years to come, that of developing an admissions policy that would be fair and equitable.

School enrolment policy

The Education Act (1998) requires schools to develop and publish an admissions policy, more commonly known as the school's Enrolment Policy. This document sets out the procedures whereby children are admitted to the school. It also sets out the procedures which schools must follow where the number of applications for admission exceeds the number of places available. In the case of Mary, Mother of Hope National School, we were faced with a huge dilemma. As a Catholic school, established under the patronage of the Archbishop of Dublin, we were very clearly aware of the need to uphold the Catholic ethos of the school and were anxious to so do. Section 15 of the Education Act legally requires schools to uphold the ethos of the school and is unequivocal in how it requires Boards of Management to:

> uphold, and be accountable to the patron for so upholding, the characteristic spirit of the school as determined by the cultural, educational, moral, religious, social, linguistic and spiritual values and traditions which inform and are characteristic of the objectives and conduct of the school. (Section 15(2)(b))

As such, there was a clear expectation that the Board of Management would adopt an enrolment policy that would prioritise children with a Catholic baptism certificate over children without one, in the event of the school not having enough school places to meet demand. Catholic schools throughout the country had adopted such a model for the admission of pupils, with little public attention or scrutiny. It is only when schools are oversubscribed and are forced to turn pupils away that the inherent difficulties with such policies become evident. In our community, due to the changing demographics of Dublin 15, this issue would become explosive.

Ethnic diversity

Many of the burgeoning estates in the area were built prior to the property bubble of the past decade. As the property market began to heat, many families moved out to estates in the Meath hinterland, while retaining their original property. Other properties were bought by investors, seeking to cash in on the property boom. Thus the houses in many of the estates went from private family-owned residences into the rental sector. The explosion of employment opportunities and the demand for more workers to feed the insatiable appetite of the Celtic Tiger brought many workers from across Europe and further afield to Dublin 15. The availability of affordable housing and the high number of rental properties meant that the area became an attractive location for this new workforce. This period of economic migration was accompanied by a huge increase in the number of people entering the country under the asylum system. Many of these families also set up home in Dublin 15. The net result of these patterns of immigration was that by the 2006 census, 27 per cent of the 90,043 enumerated in Dublin 15 classified themselves as 'other than White Irish' (Central Statistics Office, 2008). In some parts of Dublin 15, including the area where our school is located, that figure is significantly higher.

In our community in Littlepace, the ethnic diversity of the 'New Ireland' was clearly visible, with up to 50 per cent of those seeking places in the school from newcomer backgrounds. Many of these families were from a diversity of religious faiths and many of no faith. Therefore, the application of the orthodox admissions policy of 'Catholics first' would, quite literally, have split the community along religious and ethnic grounds. The children from Irish backgrounds were almost exclusively Catholic and white. They would have priority access to the available school places at the expense of the non-Catholic applicants who were almost exclusively from newcomer backgrounds.

The politics of exclusion

From a legislative perspective, it seemed clear that the school *could* apply such a divisive policy and have the full protection of the law. The Equal Status Act 2000 allowed for such discrimination, where the objective of the school is 'to provide education in an environment which promotes certain religious values'. In the case of Catholic schools, therefore, the act suggested that it was permissible for schools to give priority to Catholic children over non-Catholic. However, this presented me with huge moral difficulty, and this issue became my most significant leadership challenge as principal. I believed passionately that our school should provide a focal point around which this fledgling community should grow and develop. How then, I asked, could we aspire to such a vision if our first act as a school and a Board of Management was to exclude the children from newcomer backgrounds who were living in the community and develop a school which would become, over time, exclusively white, Irish and Catholic?

Issues around enrolment policy became an increasingly vexed topic of conversation at our local principal support meetings. Most of the schools in the area were under Catholic patronage. Many had adopted the traditional 'Catholics first' model for prioritising places. Others had used the 'chronological age' criteria, whereby all applicants, regardless of their religious background, were included in the pool for enrolment, and places were offered on age basis, starting with the oldest children and moving down the list until all places were offered. After endless hours of debate, deliberation and consultation on the matter, this was the model adopted by our Board of Management. We felt that it was a fairer and more equitable manner of offering school places. It did not split new entrants to the school on religious and racial grounds and ensured that the ethnic composition of the school was broadly in line with that of the community.

Once the Board had agreed on the criteria that we would use to enrol pupils, we then had to turn our attention to the fact that we were massively oversubscribed for school places. In 2005, for example, we had up to 240 pupils applying for just 120 school places. This resulted in half of our applicants being turned away and, because we were using the chronological age criterion, we were forced to refuse to enrol children who were up to four years and nine months old. This caused untold anxiety for parents in the area and in turn became a major political issue. Catholic parents complained that it was their right to a Catholic education and that the school was denying them that right by allowing older, non-Catholic children to enrol in the school. Equally, younger siblings of children enrolled in the school were not able to secure a place because of the cut-off date. The refusal to enrol was challenged by parents, using the appeals process set out in Section 29 of the Education Act. Although the school successfully defended these appeals, the process was hugely stressful for myself and other Board members.

The school Board of Management felt this pressure acutely. We physically hadn't the space to take any more children. The Planning Section in the Department was hopelessly ill-equipped to deal with the crisis. While construction for our first 16-classroom building was delayed because of funding difficulties, we were already in negotiation with the Department to build a second school building of the same size. Meanwhile prefabs were sprouting up all over the campus. Parents of children who had been refused enrolment in the school and who felt justifiably aggrieved started an active campaign of protest. All of this was played out under the full glare of the media – television camera crews arrived at the school to observe the queues for school places, there was blanket coverage of the 'Dublin 15' schools crisis on TV and the radio. Dealing with and responding to media enquiries was a new addition to my job description! The matter was raised repeatedly in the Dáil; parliamentary questions were placed and on one occasion details of confidential talks between the school Board of Management and the DES were disclosed in an adjournment debate in the Dáil, much to the displeasure of those of us who were involved in the negotiations.

This chaotic and oftentimes shambolic approach to planning had a hugely negative effect on our community. The acute shortage of school places – which by 2005 was being felt all over Dublin 15 – caused trauma to individual families but also threatened to damage community relations. Research from social psychology would suggest that racial tensions in mixed communities are heightened when there is a perceived shortage of resources, be it scarcity of housing or employment opportunities. One of the most precious resources for a family, one could suggest, is securing a school place for the children in the household. Therefore the shortage of school places contributed to a heightening of racial discord that could have been avoided if the correct planning procedures were put in place. This was the backdrop against which we sought to build an inclusive and welcoming school, and the 'intercultural dimension' to education became a focus for Mary, Mother of Hope National School.

Responding to the challenge

The migrant community in Ireland is a very diverse group. The 2006 census found over 180 nationalities represented in the country, with over 200 languages spoken. In our school, by 2007, we had 46 nationalities represented. The most significant policy response from the DES to the multicultural and multi-ethnic society that was emerging in Ireland was the allocation of English as an Additional Language (EAL) teachers to schools. By 2008 the number of EAL teachers at primary level exceeded 1,600. In our school, these teachers were deployed to assist pupils who had little or no spoken English. However, it soon became clear that the needs of our newcomer children were complex and not solely language based. Newcomers in our school are not a homogeneous group and, while some children settled in quite well, others found the early settling in period stressful and challenging. Like many other schools across the country, we were on a steep learning curve. Many of our newcomer children had not been to playschool, some because it was too expensive and others because there were not enough preschool places. This added to the initial settling in difficulties for the children. EAL teachers were deployed in classrooms to provide in-class support alongside the class teacher. There was a strong initial focus on socialisation, settling the children in to the routine of school life.

Because immigration to the country was such a recent phenomenon, the DES was ill-equipped to assist schools in meeting the challenges. Many of the early practices and policies that emerged were developed from the ground up and, as schools started to recover from the initial shock that immigration had presented, they began developing more focused responses to the challenges. Across Dublin 15, school principals began to share their experiences and their difficulties. Shared conversations between school principals around their frustration at the lack of an adequate policy response from the DES led school principals in Dublin 15 to commission research on the matter. I was fortunate enough to secure a secondment to St Patrick's College, Drumcondra, to carry out the fieldwork for the research and along with Dr Ciarán

Sugrue, from St Patrick's College, produced the report *Intercultural Education: Primary Challenges in Dublin 15* in 2007 (McGorman and Sugrue, 2007). The report catalogued the experiences of schools in Dublin 15 as they sought to come to terms with the new realities that immigration had presented. It documented the perspectives of teachers, principals, parents and pupils in school across Dublin 15. It also challenged stakeholders – from the DES to school patrons and wider society – to critically review policy on immigration and integration. It was a hugely rewarding experience for me personally and, hopefully, added to the national conversation that was beginning to emerge around interculturalism and the type of society we wished to develop.

School patronage and inclusion

At the time of the publication of the Dublin 15 research, there was much discussion and controversy around the issue of school patronage, which continues to the present. Because of the shortage of school places in the Diswellstown area of Dublin 15, Scoil Choilm was established in 2007 as an emergency school. This school would become the first of a new model of schools, known as Community National Schools, which would operate under the patronage of the local Vocational Educational Committee. These schools would be charged with providing equality of access for children of all faiths and none and would offer, where possible, religious instruction during the school day to children of the different faiths represented within the school population. To date, five such schools have opened. These schools are still in the early stages of development and are being closely observed to see how effectively they establish themselves as *community* national schools, serving and being supported by the whole community in which they are established.

The issue of school patronage is a complex one. The dominance of the Catholic church, which is patron of 91 per cent of primary schools in the state, has been challenged. Educate Together has emerged as the patron body which has opened the greater number of new schools within the past five years. Community National schools will, it seems, also play a significant role in future provision. However, it is the attitude and behaviour of the Catholic Bishops, who are patrons of the majority of the schools, that will be critical in determining how the intercultural agenda is played out in the coming years. It has been suggested by the Catholic hierarchy, led by the Archbishop of Dublin, Dr Diarmuid Martin, that some Catholic schools might be *divested* of Catholic patronage, in accordance with the wishes of local communities. In August 2010, the DES published a document identifying areas where the Catholic church could potentially divest its patronage of certain primary schools (DES, 2010). This would reduce the number of Catholic schools and, in theory at least, allow for more plurality of provision.

However, such developments would not necessarily lead to greater inclusion. In the event of the number of Catholic schools reducing, there is a risk that such schools, adhering to a 'Catholic first' enrolment policy, would become even more exclusive, more Catholic and, as a result, less likely to reflect the diversity of the communities in which they are established. As a further consequence, other schools, attached to other patrons, would become schools for 'the other', dividing communities, increasing their sense of exclusion and creating the potential for a two-tier education system. This would surely not be in the interest of inclusion. The challenge – and I would argue the moral duty – for all schools, but especially for Catholic schools, who are the majority provider in the state, is to critically examine their policies and practices with regard to enrolment, and to make certain that they are revised to ensure that they are inclusive and allow access to all the children of the community. Perhaps this is how they can best serve their communities and help to ensure that they meet the new challenges emerging in the New Ireland.

References

Central Statistics Office (2008) *Census 2006: Non-Irish Nationals Living in Ireland*. Dublin: The Stationery Office.

Department of Education and Skills (2010) *Information on Areas for Possible Divesting of Patronage of Primary Schools*. Available at: www.education.ie/servlet/blobservlet/report_divesting_of_patronage_primary_schools.pdf

Education Act (1998) Dublin: The Stationery Office. Available at: http://www.irishstatutebook.ie/1998/en/act/pub/0051/index.html

Equal Status Act (2000) Dublin: The Stationery Office. Available at: http://www.irishstatutebook.ie/2000/en/act/pub/0008/index.html

McGorman, E. and Sugrue, C. (2007) *Intercultural Education: Primary Challenges in Dublin 15*. Available at: http://www.spd.dcu.ie/main/news/documents/InterculturalEducationReport.pdf

Martin Wallace

A new school for a new century

The 1990s was an important decade in Irish education from a leadership perspective. Early in the decade a Green Paper was published which viewed the principal as a manager of resources and people rather than a leading teacher. One of the six aims of the Green Paper was 'To make the best use of education resources – by radically devolving administration, introducing the best management practice and strengthening policy making' (Rialtas na hEireann, 1992: 5). The principal as CEO is envisaged as playing a pivotal role in the implementation of this aim. The Green Paper's view of the principal proved contentious and a different view was expressed by The National Education Convention that followed.

The Report of The National Convention published in 1994 gives a detailed account of what many consider to be a watershed in Irish education. It highlights the view that the research literature consistently identifies good leadership as one of the key factors of successful schools. Key elements of the role of principal are stated as follows:

> The successful principal is seen as providing skilled instructional leadership for the staff, a supportive school climate, with particular emphasis on the curriculum and teaching and directed towards maximising academic learning, having clear goals and high expectations for staff and students, establishing good systems for monitoring student performance and achievement, promoting ongoing staff development and in-service and encouraging strong parental involvement and identification with and support for the school. (Convention Secretariat, 1994: 42)

The participants at the convention held the view that 'Instructional leadership was the most neglected aspect of the principal's work in the school. Pressure of time, with the urgent taking precedence over the important, and insufficient back-up support services were cited as the main reasons for the neglect' (ibid.: 43). While the report agrees that good leadership is essential for effectiveness and highlights the importance of the principal creating a supportive school climate, it is unclear as to the exact role of the principal as leader of the school. Is the principal the leading teacher, the manager, or a chief executive? Equally, is the relationship between principal and staff participatory and democratic or bureaucratic and managerialist? These were questions I was asking myself during this period as I strove to become an effective school leader.

During this decade I worked as a deputy principal and principal in two different schools. The experiences gained through my work in these positions, together with knowledge gained from reading and research, led me to apply for a position of principal in a new 800-student Greenfield school in the autumn of 1999. On 1 January 2000 when I, along with the rest of the world, celebrated the beginning of the new millennium, I was also privately celebrating my appointment as principal of Castletroy College. This was a school which, on that day, had no students, no staff and no building but did have a supportive local community and a local education authority, County Limerick VEC, which played a pivotal role in supporting me and the school in many essential areas. As principal of a new school I was fully cognisant of the responsibility and the opportunity that had been given to me. Four years previously on my first day as a school principal, a teacher had expressed the wish that I would be successful in the job. He said, 'If you are successful as principal of this school then the school will be a success and my preference is to work in a successful school.' I also believed that good leadership is a key feature of a successful school but leadership and schools as organisations can be viewed in different ways. I knew that I needed to be clear in my views and that my primary role as principal was to create and nurture a culture of teaching and learning in a happy, safe and inclusive environment.

Meeting parents of prospective students

The builder was due to commence work in February around the same time as the local second level schools' closing date for enrolment of new students for the next academic year. I met parents on an individual basis, answered their questions, allayed their concerns and outlined my views as to what the school would be like. The concerns of parents were many; the more prominent being, Would the building be completed on time? What intake policy would the school adopt? Would the teaching be of a high standard? What size would the school ultimately become? What subjects would the school offer? How would the classes be formed?

It was critical that I had a clear view as to what the school would be like and that it was based on sound educational principles and where necessary was supported by evidence from educational research, particularly in the areas of mixed-ability teaching and co-education. Many of the parents' experiences were of single-sex schools and classes which were streamed both in their own time at school and in the schools of their older children. When a minority of parents wondered why we would not have a best class, I replied it was so that we would not have a worst class. I firmly believe that a school should serve all the children of the local community regardless of academic ability or social background and I articulated this view as a starting point for the creation of our school vision. I also emphasised that the curriculum would offer a comprehensive range of subjects and that it would be determined by the students' choice of subjects. The timetable and class structure would allow both for subject choice and choice of level through the setting of Irish, English and Mathematics and Languages.

I strongly believe that a school should be values driven rather than systems driven as I, along with many principals, am concerned about the undue influence of the examination and points regime in Irish second level education. In articulating the view that Castletroy College would be a school that valued effort and improvement, that it would be child centred, emphasising the holistic development of the student, I was offering my own view as well as that of the Board of Management. At all times I was conscious that the vision I was promoting was a shared vision which would be a challenge for some people but would be acceptable to many people. It is not possible for a school to be all things to all men or women but a compelling vision based on sound values and beliefs connected to teaching and learning is an essential prerequisite to a successful future for any school.

Recruitment and induction

It was clear that all new members of staff, both teaching and non-teaching, would be involved from the outset in the school's destiny and consequently great importance was attached to the recruitment process. Every effort was made to offer a full range of subjects to the incoming first year students and it was necessary to recruit a mixture of full-time and part-time staff in order to accommodate this objective. Regardless of employment status we sought people who valued doing a good job within a team environment: people who were willing to use their own initiative, to embrace change, who were child centred and, in the case of teachers, were committed to the process of teaching and learning in an inclusive and mixed-ability environment.

The Board of Management had identified 'The education of the individual as a whole person' as the mission for the school and it was my role to facilitate the building of a philosophy, ethos and, in time, an identity to realise this mission. I felt that the best way to achieve this aim was to nurture a culture of openness which would promote participation and partnership, and value change and innovation. To this end I used the metaphor of being members of a jazz band rather than an orchestra. While we were all playing the same tune it was not set in stone and there was plenty of scope for improvisation and taking on an identifiable leadership role as the need arose and as one's talents allowed.

These matters were discussed at the first induction day, which was held in May. That day was central to the process of a shared understanding of what the future held. From the outset it was important that we knew where we were going and that we were all willing to share the responsibility of getting there. I expressed the wish that I would be a wise, consistent and corrective principal rather than being overpowering, rigid and controlling. It was agreed that we had an opportunity to be creative and innovative within the confines of a national curriculum. It was also accepted by all that we had an enormous responsibility to build a school which reflected the wishes of parents and the local community, who had fought for many years to achieve this objective.

We were aware that the challenge involved in starting a new school, one that was to grow organically over the next six years, also brought with it responsibilities and opportunities. Opportunities for staff were considered in the context of a school organisation that would encourage personal growth and development and would in particular welcome:

- independent thought and action;
- participation in setting goals;
- authority and responsibility connected with posts of responsibility.

Open communications

The importance of a clear system of communication was also raised and it was readily accepted that the norm of one staff meeting per term was not sufficient, particularly in the context of a new school. The importance of open and clear systems of communication would, we believed, build a climate of trust, encourage the flow of ideas and assist in coordinating our work. It was agreed that a weekly meeting would be our choice and this was arranged by reducing each class period on a Tuesday by five minutes. This weekly meeting proved invaluable as a means of information gathering and dispersal as well as providing time for subject and whole school planning. It also assisted in building a team spirit as discussions were invariably positive and each person's commitment was evident by their willingness to offer suggestions and to participate in new initiatives.

In addition weekly meetings are held by the Senior Pastoral Care Team, the Junior Pastoral Care Team and the Student Support Team. The value of these regular timetabled meetings cannot be underestimated as they primarily deal with student welfare issues and are proactive in nature. The Student Support Team deals with students, often someone who is experiencing a crisis in his or her life outside of school. The members of this team receive regular in-service through the vocational education committee (VEC) and the HSE.

When a student died tragically this team was an invaluable resource as each member had a specific role to fulfil in the context of a school crisis. It was widely acknowledged that the existence of this support team helped greatly in assisting all who were grief-stricken by the event.

Empowerment

If a key aspect of successful leadership is the wise use of power, then an appropriate management structure is critical to sharing that power and ensuring that the work of the school in pastoral care, curriculum development and administration is efficient and effective. Empowerment facilitates the creation of a supportive school climate while developing the leadership potential of the people involved. Delegation at one extreme has been referred to as simply 'passing the buck', but in reality by devolving authority and responsibility leadership is distributed throughout the organisation, giving teachers opportunities to be creative in areas other than teaching while showing students that a team effort is our preferred choice. We were also recognising that as the school grew bigger it would not be possible for a limited number of people to manage what would be considered to be a large organisation, both internally and externally.

The initial filling of management positions occurred over the first five years of the school's existence as the number of posts of responsibility was contingent on the size of the school. Some of the initial duties attached to the posts were relevant to the needs of a new and growing school. When a review of the posts of responsibility took place it was decided to re-prioritise some duties to meet new needs. The review took place through the School Development Planning Initiative and was a very worthwhile process, which created a new schedule of posts showing a greater emphasis on the pastoral dimension of our role as educators.

Developing a mission statement

The original mission statement as outlined by the first Board of Management, 'The education of the individual as a whole person', underpinned our work for the first five years and saw expression in successes of our students both in the academic and extra-curricular activities dimensions of education. In year five, when the school had reached its capacity and a full cohort of staff had been recruited, it was an opportune time to look at our mission statement and review it in the context of what we were actually doing and to ensure that it reflected the shared view of the purposes of the school.

At a time when there was, and still is, a danger that market forces could dominate the education agenda, with the inherent danger that the only criterion for success is exam results – results which are often generated by forms of assessment that can hinder good teaching and learning – it was considered important that we should continue to show that we wished to contribute to the development of the whole person as a member of a community that is both multicultural and multi-denominational. The resultant mission statement reads as follows:

> Our mission is the holistic education of the individual, enabling students to become responsible, caring members of society as well as encouraging them to reach their full potential.
>
> In our daily lives we value the principles of justice and mutual respect embracing all denominations and cultures. We endeavour to nurture and maintain a school community, which involves the partnership of staff, students, parents, trustees and the local community.
>
> In pursuit of this ideal we provide a broad and balanced range of curricular and extra-curricular experiences for all students.

Conclusion

In the past ten years Castletroy College has grown to a school of over one thousand students. The school has built an extension to cater for the demographic growth in the local area. The students of the college have achieved admirable results in both academic and non-academic endeavours. College teams have come to national prominence in basketball, rugby and soccer, while individual students have excelled in the Young Scientist Competition, international swimming and athletics events.

During this period an annual programme of continuing professional development has taken place concentrating on teaching and learning in an inclusive environment. Topics such as differentiation, team teaching, personalising learning and assessment for learning have received particular attention. Members of staff have been seconded to Department of Education initiatives such as Leadership Development, Special Education Support, Project Maths and T4. In 2010 the school was selected as one of 78 schools to receive a 100 megabits broadband connection, while all classrooms were equipped with a multimedia projector. The school has developed its own virtual learning environment using the Moodle platform.

A number of subject inspections have taken place, which have acknowledged and affirmed the work of the teachers and students while also offering recommendations for improvement. The most recent inspection was in the area of Special Education and we were particularly pleased that the report of the inspection strongly commended the whole-school approach in this area, as one of the values that guides our daily lives is that of meeting the needs of the most vulnerable in our school while encouraging all students to achieve their goals.

References

Convention Secretariat (1994) Report On The National Education Convention. Dublin: Government Publications.

Rialtas Na hEireann (1992) 'Education For A Changing World'. Green Paper. Dublin: Government Publications.

Part III

The Developing Picture

Chapter 11

Rethinking Educational Leadership

John West-Burnham

Abstract

This chapter argues for a shift in thinking about the nature of school leadership. It starts by questioning the relevance and appropriateness of traditional models of organisational design to schools. In particular it challenges the application of rational-bureaucratic models to schools and then goes on to review the possible implications of this approach for learners and learning. The chapter then moves into the development of a possible alternative approach by considering the concept of community as a possible model for school structure, culture and relationships. The central hypothesis of the chapter is that the theory and practice of community is a more appropriate paradigm for learning and well-being than traditional organisational structures and processes. Criteria for the components of social capital are outlined and these are then considered in detail in terms of their implications for definitions of effective leadership. The chapter closes by considering the implications of the potential tension between bureaucratising the curriculum and creating a learning community.

Key words

Educational leadership; organisation theory; school improvement; effective schools; rational-legal models; bureaucracy; community; social capital; transforming schools.

In the continuing debate about the nature and future of educational leadership there are many caricatures and polarities. One of the most abiding is the contrast between the managerial principal, dressed in a designer suit, with abundant personal technology and replete with plans, strategies and models of preferred outcomes. On the other hand is the tweed-jacketed, elbow-patched principal who only feels truly comfortable when teaching, likes children, and has difficulty distinguishing an iPod from an iPhone, not to mention the iPad. Of course, it is easy to caricature but there is a real cultural divide in many education systems:

> For the new manager in education, good management involves the smooth and efficient implementation of aims set outside the school, within constraints also set outside the school. It is not the job of the new manager to question or criticise these aims and constraints. The new management discourse in education empha-sises the instrumental purposes of schooling – raising standards and performance as measured by examination results, levels of attendance and school leaver destinations – and is frequently articulated within a lexicon of enterprise, excellence, quality and effectiveness. (Gerwitz, 2002: 32)

This chapter will review some of the prevailing assumptions about the nature of organisations, and the leadership of those organisations and how that relates to models of schools and schooling. It will also consider the extent to which it is possible to reconcile prevailing models of effective organisations with the nature of education and learning. Sergiovanni is direct and robust in his challenge:

> ... in trying to understand what drives leadership, we have overem-phasized bureaucratic, psychological and technical rational author-ity, seriously neglecting professional and moral authority ... The result has been a leadership literature that borders on vacuity and a leadership practice that is not leadership at all. (Wheatley, 1992: 3)

In a number of education systems around the world the increasing focus on school autonomy, site-based management and increasing competition may have had the result of exacerbating Sergiovanni's concerns. Wheatley's optimism in 1992 seems somewhat premature, at least as far as schools are concerned:

> Our concept of organizations is moving away from the mechanistic creations that flourished in the age of bureaucracy. We have begun to speak in earnest of more fluid organic structures, even of bound-aryless organizations. We are beginning to recognize organizations as systems, construing them as 'learning organizations' and crediting them with some type of self-renewing capacity. (Wheatley, 1992: 13)

Now, of course, it may be that the issue is as much a matter of cultural identity as prevailing management thinking and organisation theory. There is a very strong case that much of the managerialism in school leadership writing comes from the American/English/ Australian axis and as such it should be treated with great caution by other cultures. For example; the Celtic nations, the Breton, Cornish, Irish, Manx, Welsh and Scots peoples, appear to an outsider to place greater stress on kinship and community and to be less deferential to central government and more committed to a cultural and historical identity. This may in part be attributable to the Norman conquest of England that saw the rapid acceptance of an alien culture by the indigenous English to the extent that within 50 years of the (totally illegal) Norman invasion Saxon names and culture had been largely eradicated. The Normans were the precursors of modern bureaucracy, hierarchy and centralised control – which the Celtic nations resisted and continue to resist rather more successfully than the English. There is a real danger of cultural imperialism at work here with spurious attempts to create an international hegemony about effective leadership.

Schools as organisations

A first, and key, issue is the extent to which a school is an organisation. It seems very difficult to equate the local post-primary school with a multinational business, let alone a two-teacher primary school in the remotest parts of County Kerry. All sorts of variables explain the differences between different types of organisation, of which size, purpose and culture are pivotal factors. However, it is possible to identify certain common factors that can serve to analyse any type of human endeavour. This process of analysis is probably best known as organisation theory and it is not intended to summarise its full range here. What is useful is the dominant perspective of organisations derived from the Weberian legal-rational model that is usually expressed as the organisation as bureaucracy with the following characteristics (Bush, 2003: 44):

- The structure is hierarchical with authority derived from the place of the individual in the 'chain of command'. Each level in the hierarchy is accountable to the level above with rewards and sanctions available.

- The organisation is 'goal oriented' with senior leaders responsible for defining goals and obtaining commitment and compliance to them.

- Work is allocated on the basis of a division of labour that is derived from specialization of expertise or knowledge.
- The work of the organisation is largely determined by rules, standards, procedures that emphasize the need for conformity and consistency.
- Relationships are impersonal with an emphasis on formality and relative status.
- Appointment, promotion and career development are based on explicit public criteria and transparent procedures.

These criteria appear in numerous permutations and with a wide range of cultural interpretations but over and over again they are accepted, often uncritically, as the norm of organisational life. Crucially for this discussion elements of these criteria can be found in educational institutions of all types.

> Scholars of organizations decided to set aside substantive rationality, morality, politics or ideology, and to focus on the search for techniques that link ends and means in the most efficient way. In this view, human action is a subset of 'instrumental rationality' alone, as it is subordinated to unspecified and transient 'external' objectives ... Choosing one side of the equation, as organization theorists have done elevates instrumental rationality to a supreme position that gainsays attempts at critical assessment. (Shenhav, 2003: 200)

In terms of education policy in developed countries the emphasis has been on the related outcomes of improvement and effectiveness, both of which are expressed in terms of various types of performance. In essence the emphasis is on schools qua organisations boosting effectiveness, efficiency and outcomes, largely through quantitative measures. While there will be numerous counter-examples most schools, even the smallest, will have elements of the bureaucratic model – often, it has to be conceded, the result of central and local government imposition. However, so many aspects of the ways schools work are so deeply embedded in bureaucratic principles that it is easy to forget the extent to which they are 'taken for granted' assumptions.

In many ways schooling might be thought of as an essentially rectangular process:

- The architectural plan of a school is essentially a series of rectangles.
- The arrangement of desks in classrooms is a permutation of rectangles.

- Lessons are often planned as linear blocks.

- Schooling is based on a linear curriculum arranged in subject blocks.

- Advancement through the school system is by automatic chronological cohort progression. (West-Burnham, 2010a: 58)

Schools thrive on bureaucracy and remain one of the most formal of organisational settings. For example, consider the issue of automatic chronological cohort progression – the strategy by which children move through the school according to age and their membership of a particular cohort rather than any individual needs. Any primary school teacher will know that in a given class there will be a wide range of ability, chronological age is no measure of cognitive development, and yet, in spite of demonstrable heterogeneity, the class moves as a body; a triumph of procedures and structures over the needs of the individual child. There are similar manifestations of this issue in the design of the school day, the nature of the curriculum experience and the issues outlined by Hargreaves below. These examples might be seen to confirm the proposition that schools are essentially rational formal organisations.

> Formal models assume that organizations are hierarchical systems in which managers use rational means to pursue agreed goals. Heads possess authority legitimized by their formal positions within the organizations and are accountable to sponsoring bodies for the activities of their institutions. (Bush, 2003: 37)

Of course, no school works in this way all the time; early years provision will have a fundamentally different culture to the very large post-primary school or vocational college – 'formal models remain valid as *partial* descriptions of organisation and management in education' (Bush, 2003: 59). However, even in the most explicitly child-centred environment most of the characteristics listed above will be found. What seems to happen is that, as children get older, so they are formally inducted into contributing to making the school operate as a formal organisation. While all sorts of 'softening' strategies may ameliorate this, the fact remains that for many – students, their parents and the staff – schools are places that have to be engaged with on the organisation's terms.

> Human beings live and work in such organizations, but we feel like passive units of production. Our lives serve the organizations, but the organization serves only our utilitarian needs. (Zohar, 1997: 5)

Table 11.1 Educational imaginaries (after Hargreaves, 2004: 30–32)

19th-century educational imaginary	21st-century educational imaginary
Students are prepared for a fixed situation in life.	Students' identities and destinations are fluid.
Intelligence is fixed.	Intelligence is multidimensional.
Schools are culturally homogeneous.	Schools are heterogeneous.
Schools of a type are interchangeable.	Schools of a type are diverse.
Schooling is limited for the majority.	Education provides personalised learning for all.
Schools have rigid and clear boundaries.	Education is lifelong for every student.
Schools work on the factory model.	Education is unconstrained by time and place.
Roles are sharply defined and segregated.	Roles are blurred and overlapping.
Schools and teachers work autonomously.	Educators work in complex networks.
Education is producer led.	Education is user led.

Schools are intriguing in that in a world that is increasingly challenging the integrity and validity of the formal, rational organisation they remain islands of hierarchy and bureaucracy. Although it is almost at the level of a banality it probably is true to say that schools are one of the few surviving vestiges of the 19th century. In Hargreaves' very powerful model (see Table 11.1) it is easy to see that the 19th-century imaginary (the prevailing hegemony, the dominant norms and expectations of most people) remains deeply influential with only some minor concessions to the 21st century.

The 19th-century imaginary was seamlessly adopted for the 20th century and still has a significant hold over a range of perceptions as to how schools should work. However, even the most cursory analysis points to a substantial change in the context in which schools function and the nature of the society they serve. The combined effects of secularisation and consumerism have served to change many of the a priori assumptions that determine how modern European societies work. Changing patterns of family and community life and profound shifts in the nature of employment point to very different contexts for schools. The 19th-century imaginary is essentially a product of a different world order. As Zohar describes:

We live largely in a world of Newtonian organizations. These are organizations that thrive on certainty and predictability. They are hierarchical; power emanates from the top, and control is vital at every level. So, often, is fear. They are heavily bureaucratic and rule-bound, and hence inflexible. They stress the single point of view, the one best way forward. (Zohar, 1997: 5)

In spite of this I would suggest that much educational policymaking, the design and delivery of the curriculum, the spatial and learning architecture of schools and the organisation of human relationships are essentially based on a 19th-century imaginary, rooted in a Newtonian world and articulated through the language of scientific management and legal-rational systems. This combination of factors makes for a very complex conceptual framework – an imaginary that is so deeply embedded in our collective world view that we may be inclined to see it as the world – rather than one interpretation of it. Just as in Plato's allegory of the cave, we may have been so habituated into one view of organisations that we believe that they are organisations – in the same way that shadows were perceived as reality.

However, when we look at the reality in which schools and all other social institutions are now operating, then the prevailing imaginary and its various iterations are increasingly inappropriate:

It is no longer possible to rely on linear models of management. Linear models of management, which underpinned the simple linear causality of the command and control mentality of hierarchical, bureaucratic organizations, have to be replaced with networked, nonlinear, emergent, mutually informing groups. (Morrison, 2002: 16)

There are many ways of conceptualising the tension between the competing paradigms of the linear and non-linear, for example modern and postmodern. One radically different way of conceptualising the tension has been developed by MacGilchrist (2009) in a unique and compelling argument. In essence he explores various ways of interpreting and explaining the world from one of the most fundamental perspectives – our neurological functioning, in particular how the two hemispheres in our brains influence how we perceive and engage with the world.

The world of the left hemisphere, dependent on denotative language and abstraction, yields clarity and power to manipulate things that are known, fixed, static, isolated, decontextualised, explicit, disembodied, general in nature but ultimately lifeless. (MacGilchrist, 2009: 174)

As might be expected he views the right hemisphere in a very different way, arguing that it

... yields a world of individual, changing, evolving, interconnected, implicit, incarnate, living beings within the context of the lived world, but in the nature of things never fully graspable, always imperfectly known – and to this world it exists in a relationship of care. (2009: 174)

What would happen if the left hemisphere became dominant in the world?

Fewer people would find themselves doing work involving contact in the real 'lived' world rather than plans, strategies, paperwork, management and bureaucratic procedures. In fact more and more work would come to be overtaken by the meta-process of documenting or justifying what one was doing or supposed to be doing – at the expense of the real job in the real world. (2009: 429)

This last point would probably be echoed by school leaders across the world – how much time is diverted from doing 'the real job in the real world'? But it is actually worse than that because in the absence of real moral confidence and clarity of purpose then it is possible to forget the real job and engage in surrogate activities.

From organisation to community

In an increasingly complex world, which shows every sign of increasing in complexity, it may be that an alternative paradigm to the legal-rational bureaucratic model is required.

Complex adaptive systems possess a capability for self-organization which enables them to develop, extend, replace, adapt, reconstruct or change their internal structure (or modus operandi) so that they can respond to and influence their environment. (Morrison, 2002: 14)

Table 11.2 offers a model to help explore the differences between the formal bureaucratic paradigm and an alternative model based on the characteristics identified by Morrison above; by a range of criteria this points to the idea of moving from organisations to communities as the dominant conceptual model. Obviously such a list is value-laden and contains a range of implicit assumptions. Equally it would be wrong to see the two columns as polarised opposites; each of the criteria needs to be seen as part of a continuum. In his discussion of Linux, the open-source software community, Leadbeater (2003: 41) argues that innovative communities

... seem to combine many ingredients that are traditionally kept separate, or at least prove difficult to combine. There is healthy competition within the community but also cooperation and sharing; it thrives on masses of individual initiative but is founded on a public good, ... the community is highly distributed and virtual, yet also hierarchical, with a single authority at its heart.

Table 11.2 therefore needs to be seen as a continuum with a wide range of possible permutations.

The nature and relationships of the elements defined in Table 11.2 will be explored in the following discussion and commentary. Many readers will recognise the manifestations of the organisational perspective in school life outlined in the left-hand column in Table 11.2. The focus on control, obedience and hierarchy may have been culturally acceptable at one time but it seems unlikely that it did much to facilitate effective learning and the development of human potential. It is a matter to be widely debated but by a number of criteria organisations tend to work, ultimately, through power. Communities work through consent based on shared moral or personal authority. Power is the ultimate manifestation of the immature organisation.

Another factor is size or scale. Dunbar (2010) has produced very powerful arguments to reinforce his claim that somewhere around 150 people is the natural unit of human interaction and engagement. It would seem to make sense to use Dunbar's number as the basis for social organisation. He tells the story of GoreTex, the clothing company that underwent a period of significant success; rather than

Table 11.2   From organisation to community

Organisation	Community
Competition	Collaboration
Hierarchy	Networks
Obedience	Consent/consensus
Certainty/linearity	Complexity/uncertainty
Top-down power	Shared authority
Low trust/control	High trust
Specialisation/boundaries	Interdependent working
Career structure	Personal growth pathways
Efficiency/outcomes	Enhanced value
Performance-based accountability	Moral accountability
Rule-bound	Value-driven

expand the existing sites the company's founder created additional units of about 150:

> By keeping his factory units below the critical size of 150 he was able to do away with hierarchies and management structures: the factory worked by personal relationships, with a sense of mutual obligation encouraging workers and managers to co-operate rather than compete. (Dunbar, 2010: 26)

In other words each factory functioned as a community. In his innovative study of the nature of the learning organisation de Geus stresses the importance of what might be seen as the human side of organisational life, the centrality of relationships and the pivotal importance of a sense of community.

> However, experience is accumulating that corporations fail because the prevailing thinking and language of management are too narrowly focused on the prevailing thinking and language of economics. To put it another way: companies die because their managers focus on the economic activity of producing goods and services, and they forget that their organization's true nature is that of a community of humans. (de Geus, 1997: 9)

According to Putnam (2000: 19):

> ... social capital refers to connections among individuals – social networks and the norms of reciprocity and trustworthiness that arise from them. In that sense social capital is closely related to what some have called 'civic virtue'. The difference is that 'social capital' calls attention to the fact that civic virtue is most powerful when embedded in a dense network of reciprocal social relations.

The best way to understand the role of social capital is to see it as a measure of the integrity of a community – the higher the level of social capital the more likely it is that an authentic community exists. Perhaps the most systematic and detailed way to define an effective community is to identify the components of social capital. There are numerous permutations available but the following elements would seem to be common to most debates around the nature of an effective community. (West-Burnham, 2010b)

Shared social norms and values: successful communities have high levels of consensus about what they believe in and how that belief is translated into day-to-day principles to live by. Obvious examples are religious communities that are characterised by a shared faith that informs the very nature of the community itself. Organisations will tend to work on acquiescence and sanctions for non-compliance rather than consent. Without being in any way facile it does seem to be the case that it is not so much a matter of what is believed, the important thing is that everybody believes in the same thing. Any community, from the smallest family to the village to a virtual community, develops a code to live by – the success of such a code is one of the first and most significant indicators of a healthy community.

Sophisticated social networks: this refers to the quality of communication in a community. In most organisations communication is essentially top down and controlled; in communities it is lateral, that is it is non-hierarchical and not subject to control via censorship or the 'chain of command'. Successful communities have a common vocabulary and opportunities for real and significant dialogue. In fact, one of the most powerful ways to help in community building is to enable multiple rich conversations that occur spontaneously.

High levels of trust: in organisational life trust is often fragile and elusive, but in many ways trust is the basis of community; what Putnam (2000) describes as bonding social capital. Bryk and Schneider (2002) describe trust as the 'connective tissue that binds schools together' and this image helps to reinforce the importance of healthy networks, neural and social, to effective learning. In essence this is all about building social capital, creating learning communities which are exemplified in the strength of social networks, interdependency, engagement, shared purpose, parity of esteem and genuine reciprocity. Covey (2006) is unambiguous about the status and role of trust in personal and community life:

> When trust is high, the dividend you receive is like a performance multiplier ... In a company high trust materially improves communication, collaboration, execution, innovation ... In your personal life, high trust significantly improves your excitement, energy, passion, creativity and joy in your relationships ... (Covey, 2006: 19)

High civic engagement: this relates to active participation and involvement in the political life of the community. This means, at the very least, voting in elections but more importantly taking an active part in community dialogue, political debate and, where appropriate, standing for office. The effective community is essentially a participative democracy where people feel that they have a genuine voice in determining their futures and the nature of their lives.

Symbols and rituals: communities celebrate their shared identity and sense of purpose. This celebration can take a wide range of forms – the football supporter wearing the team colours; the military parade; the church service; the PTA dance. In most cases these celebrations involve singing and dancing, eating together and wearing special clothes. The passion generated by Gaelic football and Irish dance is a powerful example of the importance of symbols and shared experiences in everyday life.

Interdependence and reciprocity: this means that people care about each other; they check on neighbours, they make sure that the elderly and infirm are remembered at special times; this is the story of the Good Samaritan. Communities care, and in doing so translate the moral aspiration into the daily experience. This points to collaboration rather than competition – perhaps one of the defining differences between organisational and community life.

Volunteering and community action: in highly successful communities many people serve as volunteers, in the fire department, in the school, on community projects. Volunteering is one of the most powerful indicators of high social capital because it demonstrates a level of altruism in the community and challenges the individualistic and materialistic culture.

Shared hope and aspiration: a healthy community, like an effective human being, has a sense of purpose, a sense of hope for a better future and a desire to create a better life for all members of the community. This utopian aspect of community life is often powerful social 'glue' and is very much linked to a belief in a shared future and an essential optimism.

Communities of practice: effective communities learn together, they respect and nurture wisdom and seek to build learning into every aspect of community life. In the effective community the wisdom of experience is shared, passed on and is made widely available. The focus is very much on learning in action and learning is seen as a deeply democratic process that is pragmatic and non-reverential.

Most schools will display some or most of the characteristics identified above. It may be that early years settings and primary schools are more likely to be communities as defined rather than post-primary schools. What is very obvious is that schools are at very different levels of development as communities. There are primary classrooms that are the apotheosis of formal/rational organisational structures and relationships; equally there are secondary school departments that might attribute their success to their refusal to work by organisational criteria in terms of structures and relationships.

Leadership and community

Leadership is the catalyst to enable all of the factors described above to be put into effect. The model for school leadership thus moves from running effective organisations to creating communities. Community leadership is thus about values, communication and enabling community involvement and interaction. Community leadership is based on shared leadership across the community rather than the status of a few. Leadership is based on qualities rather than qualifications, expertise rather than experience, on ability rather than seniority. This flies in the face of the norms and expectations of the rational organisation in which hierarchy is reinforced by perceived nuances of status, leadership is the culmination of a successful career progression and its success criteria will be derived from the left-hand column in Table 11.2 above. The corollary of the school as a community is school leadership as community leadership. If the criteria for effective communities identified above are accepted as the basis of a successful community then for each criterion there is a specific manifestation of leadership.

Moral leadership: if the school is to be a moral community then the leadership of that community has to be rooted in ethical principles that are translated into personal values which are then expressed in consistent moral actions. It is obviously beneficial if school leaders are able to work in a broad social hegemony. Pont et al. point out that:

> The high quality and performance of Finland's educational system cannot be divorced from the clarity, characteristics of, and broad consensus about the country's broader social vision ... There is compelling clarity about and commitment to inclusive, equitable and innovative social values beyond as well as within the educational system. (Pont et al., 2008: 80)

However, what is absolutely central is that those who hold leadership roles see themselves as stewards of a collective conscience and the medium for translating principle into practice. In a direct challenge to the worst aspects of managerialism in education Sergiovanni (1992: 4) argues:

In practice the managerial mystique represents a tacit compact among too many policymakers, administrators and academics, which places process before substance and form before function. So strongly does the mystique adhere to a belief in the right methods that the methods themselves become surrogates for results.

The result is an emphasis on doing things right, at the expense of doing the right things. In schools improvement plans become substitutes for improvement outcomes.

What constitutes the right things will always be a matter of fundamental debate given the politicisation of education in many countries.

Social networks: leadership enables networking because leaders spend a substantial proportion of their time engaged in networking and facilitating dialogue and conversations across the community. Leaders work in three ways to achieve this. Firstly they help to create a language and vocabulary for the community; secondly they see it as their role to initiate and model effective communication; and thirdly they are socially intelligent. As Goleman explains:

> Socially intelligent leadership starts with being fully present and getting in synch. Once a leader is engaged, then the full panoply of social intelligence can come into play, from sensing how people feel and why, to interacting smoothly enough to move people into a positive state. There is no magic recipe for what to do in every situation, no five-steps-to-social-intelligence-at-work. (Goleman, 2006: 280)

Trust: leadership can only function through trust; trust is the vehicle for converting leadership into followership; in other words, 'Without trust why should I follow you?' In fact I would probably be mad to do so. Bottery (2004) in his detailed and systematic analysis stresses the centrality of trust to any debate about what we are seeking to create in terms of effective societies and communities and argues that:

> ... a happy, tolerant and healthy society depends upon the blossoming of trust relationships both within communities and between them ... If the first order values of a society are not economic, but personal, social and moral, then trust has to be seen as a first order value that should be promoted for its own sake. (Bottery, 2004: 121)

Sergiovanni reinforces this point – essentially, if the values of a school are not primarily economic and it should be operating in a way that is morally valid and appropriate, then:

Leaders should be trustworthy, and this worthiness is an important virtue. Without trust leaders lose credibility. This loss poses difficulties to leaders as they seek to call people to respond to their responsibilities. The painful alternative is to be punitive, seeking to control people through manipulation or coercion. (Sergiovanni, 2005: 90)

It would be wrong to claim that communities are more likely to be built around trust than most other forms of organisation. However, it is probably entirely reasonable to claim that communities are likely to be more auspicious environments in which trust might flourish. This is explained by the culture and climate that is created by the other variables described in this section that together comprise an effective community.

Civic engagement: communities tend to be democratic. It is another manifestation of the sorts of relationships that make the difference in terms of relationships and the need for openness and interdependent living and working. Community leaders work through active participation, direct involvement in decision-taking and transparency, and doing so create a culture of shared leadership. It is now widely recognised that pupils need to be consulted in order to secure their engagement with the school as a social institution; the next step is to actively involve them in the leadership of the school. Chomsky (2000) spells out the challenge for schools:

Any school that has to impose the teaching of democracy is already suspect. The less democratic schools are, the more they need to teach about democratic ideals. If schools were really democratic, in the sense of providing opportunities for children to experience democracy through practice, they wouldn't feel the need to indoctrinate them with platitudes about democracy. (Chomsky, 2000: 27)

The implications of this last point are significant – in the school as community the learners share in the leadership in a real and non-tokenistic way.

Symbols and rituals: community leaders preside over the celebrations of community identity mentioned above. It might be the church service, the military parade, the school disco or prom or a shared celebration of the creativity and achievements of the community – it is the function of leadership to enable and enrich the sense of shared success. Whether it is the hurling final at Croke Park or the Palio in Siena, communities invest in celebrating their shared identity through wearing the colours, singing the songs and simply being together with a common purpose. Communities cohere to the extent that they sing, dance, eat and celebrate together. Schools are no different and leadership has to recognise the part it plays in giving status and significance to this aspect of community life.

Interdependence and reciprocity: perhaps one of the best ways of defining a community in contradistinction to an organisation is the degree to which it is open and engages with other communities. In Putnam's (2000) terms organisations tend to bond whereas communities tend to bond and bridge. Bonding is about creating a strong sense of identity, often based on homogeneity and a sense of being distinctive and 'different'. Bridging recognises the importance of bonding but argues that, as appropriate, there is a need to engage with other communities for mutual benefit. This moves us from the pack led by the alpha animal and the closed organisation to the open and welcoming community. The focus of leadership is collaboration; in his discussion of the Italian immigrant community of Roseto in Philadelphia Gladwell (2008) describes a community which was probably one of the healthiest in the USA at one time:

> The Rosetans were healthy because of where they were from, because of the world they had created for themselves in their tiny little town in the hills. (Gladwell, 2008: 9)

This special world was explained by:

> ... how the Rosetans visited one another, stopping to chat in Italian on the street, say, or cooking for one another in their backyards. They learned about the extended family clans that underlay the town's social structure. They saw how many homes had three generations living under one roof, and how much respect grandparents commanded. They went to mass at Our Lady of Mount Carmel and saw the unifying and calming effect of the church. They counted twenty-two separate civic organizations in a town of just under two thousand people. They picked up on the particular egalitarian ethos of the community, which discouraged the wealthy from flaunting their success and helped the unsuccessful obscure their failures. (ibid.: 9)

To understand why Roseto was so successful the researchers had to

> ... look beyond the individual. They had to understand the culture he or she was part of, and who their families and friends were, and

what town their families came from. They had to appreciate the idea that the values of the world we inhabit and the people we surround ourselves with have a profound effect on who we are. (p. 10)

Community leadership models, validates and endows community activities with status and significance.

Volunteering and community action: communities seem to work best when they are based on choice, consent and commitment. Many of the most powerful communities are based on the premise of volunteering. For example the Royal National Lifeboat Institution, a totally voluntary body that works in an entirely altruistic manner, makes the coast of Ireland and the UK safe. Perhaps the most powerful image here is that of Greenleaf's model of servant leadership that has the following components that seem to link with many of the qualities that have been discussed in previous sections:

- listening openly and receptively;
- empathy to recognise and accept others;
- healing – making whole;
- awareness – developing holistic understanding;
- persuasion – through influence, not power;
- conceptualisation – dreaming dreams;
- foresight – intuition and awareness;
- stewardship – a commitment to serving others;
- building community – collaboration and interdependence.

(Greenleaf, 1977)

Volunteering and engaging in community action are moral acts; it is the parable of the Good Samaritan and the answer to the most basic question in terms of moral and social relationships: 'Who is my neighbour?' As Hargreaves and Fink mention:

The hardest part of sustainable leadership is the part that provokes us to think beyond our own schools and ourselves. It is the part that calls us to serve the public good of all people's children within and beyond our community and not only the private interests of those who subscribe to our own institution. Sustainable leadership means caring for *all* the people our actions and choices affect – those whom we can't immediately see as well as those whom we can. ... Sustainable leadership is socially just leadership, nothing simpler, nothing less. (Hargreaves and Fink, 2006: 158)

Hope and aspiration: leaders are at their most influential and have their greatest potential impact when they are articulating hope and confidence in the future. This is primarily an emotional disposition; it means the leader is the person who is congenitally optimistic and is able to give expression to the hope, aspirations and dreams of the whole community in a way that is meaningful and motivating. This is expressed in the ambition and expectation for every child extended through to the whole community. As Vaclav Havel expresses it:

> The kind of hope that I often think about ... I understand above all as a state of mind, not a state of the world. Either we have hope within us or we don't; it is a dimension of the soul, and it's not essentially dependent on some particular observation of the world or estimate of the situation ... Hope is not the conviction that something will turn out well, but the certainty that something makes sense, regardless of how it turns out. (1990: 181)

Communities of practice: effective communities learn. In their worst manifestation organisations not only fail to learn, they are actually hostile to learning – in the way that military commanders are often accused of in preparing to fight the last war. Communities nurture wisdom; in many societies, faiths and traditions this is often manifested in the leader as storyteller, and the importance attached to community history and traditions as a way of imparting knowledge from one generation to another. Another way of understanding how this might work in organisations is Gloor's (2006) model of a COIN or collaborative innovation network. Gloor identifies the key elements of a COIN:

1 Collaboration networks are learning networks.
2 Collaboration networks need an ethical code.
3 Collaboration networks are based on trust and self-organisation.
4 Collaboration networks make knowledge accessible to everybody.
5 Collaboration networks operate in internal honesty and transparency. (Gloor, 2006: 53)

In practice these broad principles mean that collaborative networks:

> ... are self-organizing, unified by a shared vision, shared goals, and a shared value system. COIN members communicate with each other in a 'small world' networking structure where each team member can be reached quickly.

COIN members are brought together by mutual respect and a strong set of shared beliefs. These common values act as a substitute for conventional management hierarchies, directing what every COIN member 'has to do.' There is a delicate internal balance of reciprocity, and a normally unwritten code of ethics with which members of the COIN comply. (ibid.: 71)

A collaborative innovation network seems to be almost a microcosm of the effective community. It also seems to be a perfect model for both learning in a community and how learning communities such as schools might work in the future. If that is the aspiration, and it is by no means unanimous, then it might be appropriate to argue that, in the phrase of the American architect Louis Sullivan, form follows function. The challenge is to find the form of leadership that follows the function of life in a community.

Education in Ireland has a long and distinguished history. Scholarship is embedded deep in the Celtic psyche, and equally the modern history of Ireland has demonstrated a capacity for flexibility, adaptivity and responsiveness to profound demands and challenges. As with most other modern democracies the tension appears to be between state-controlled schooling and community-focused learning. Of course, these positions are not polarised, there are important elements in both, but surely education has to be at least as concerned with well-being as with performance. And, crucially, leadership has to model the sort of society we wish to become, not slavishly follow patterns and norms imposed by an alien academic hegemony.

References

Bottery, M. (2004) *The Challenges of Educational Leadership*. London: PCP.

Bryk, A.S. and Schneider, B. (2002) *Trust in Schools*. New York: Russell Sage.

Bush, T. (2003) *Theories of Educational Leadership and Management* (3rd edition). London: Sage Publications.

Chomsky, N. (2000) *Chomsky on Miseducation*. Maryland, USA: Rowman and Littlefield Publishers, Inc.

Coates, M. (ed.) (2010) *Shaping a New Educational Landscape*. London: Continuum.

Covey, Stephen M.R. (2006) *The Speed of Trust*. London: Simon and Schuster.

de Geus, A. (1997) *The Living Company*. London: Nicholas Brearley Publishing.

Dunbar, R. (2010) *How Many Friends Does One Person Need?* London: Faber and Faber.

Gerwitz, S. (2002) *The Managerial School*. London: Routledge.

Gladwell, M. (2008) *Outliers: The story of success*. London: Allen Lane.

Gloor, P.A. (2006) *Swarm Creativity*. Oxford: Oxford University Press.

Goleman, D. (2006) *Social Intelligence*. London: Hutchinson.

Greenleaf, R. (1997) *Servant Leadership*. New York: Paulist Press.

Hargreaves, A. and Fink, D. (2006) *Sustainable Leadership*. San Francisco: Jossey Bass.

Hargreaves, D. (2004) *Personalising Learning*. London: Specialist Schools Trust.

Havel, V. (1990) *Disturbing the Peace*. London: Faber and Faber.

Leadbeater, C. (2003) 'Open Innovation in Public Services', in T. Bentley and J. Wilsdon (eds), *The Adaptive State*. London: Demos.

MacGilchrist, I. (2009) *The Master and his Emissary*. New Haven and London: Yale University Press.

Morrison, K. (2002) *School Leadership and Complexity Theory*. London: Routledge Falmer.

Pont, B., Nusche, D. and Hopkins, D. (2008) *Improving School Leadership: Volume 2, Case Studies on System Leadership*. Paris: OECD.

Putnam, R. (2000) *Bowling Alone*. New York: Simon and Schuster.

Sergiovanni, T. (1992) *Moral Leadership*. San Francisco: Jossey Bass.

Sergiovanni, T. (2005) *Strengthening the Heartbeat*. San Francisco: Jossey Bass.

Shenhav, Y. (2003) 'The Historical and Epistemological Foundations of Organization Theory', in H. Tsoukas and C. Knudsen (eds), *The Oxford Handbook of Organization Theory*. Oxford: Oxford University Press.

West-Burnham, J. (2010a) 'From Schooling to Learning', in M. Coates (ed.), *Shaping a New Educational Landscape*. London: Continuum.

West-Burnham, J. (2010b) 'Educational Leadership and Social Capital', in P. Peterson, E. Baker and B. McGaw (eds), *International Encyclopedia of Education*, Volume 5, pp. 85–91. Oxford: Elsevier.

Wheatley, M. (1992) *Leadership and the New Science*. San Francisco: Berrett-Koehler Publishers.

Zohar, D. (1997) *Rewiring the Corporate Brain*. San Francisco: Berrett-Koehler Publishers.

Index

CONTEMPORARY ISSUES IN LEARNING AND TEACHING

Edited by **Margery McMahon**, **Christine Forde** and **Margaret Martin** all at *University of Glasgow*

Contemporary Issues in Learning and Teaching looks at current issues across the three key areas of policy, learning and practice. It will help you to think critically on your Education course, and to make connections between the processes of learning and the practicalities of teaching. The book addresses key issues in primary, secondary and special education, and includes examples from all four countries of the UK.

The contributors reflect on current thinking and policy surrounding learning and teaching, and what it means to be a teacher today. Looking at the practice of teaching in a wider context allows you to explore some of the issues you will face, and the evolving expectations of your role in a policy-led environment. The book focuses on core areas of debate including:

- education across different contexts and settings
- teaching in an inclusive environment
- Continuing Professional Development (CPD) for practitioners

Each chapter follows the same accessible format. They contain case studies and vignettes providing examples and scenarios for discussion; introduction and summary boxes listing key issues and concepts explored in the chapter; key questions for discussion reflection; and further reading.

This essential text will be ideal for undergraduate and postgraduate courses, including BEd//BA degrees, initial teacher-training courses, and Masters in Education programmes.

All editors and contributors are based in the Faculty of Education at Glasgow University, UK.

November 2010 • 232 pages
Cloth (978-1-84920-127-8) • £65.00
Paper (978-1-84920-128-5) • £21.99

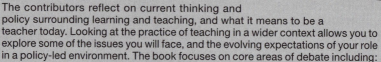

ALSO FROM SAGE

PROFESSIONALIZATION, LEADERSHIP AND MANAGEMENT IN THE EARLY YEARS

Edited by **Linda Miller** and **Carrie Cable** *both at The Open University*

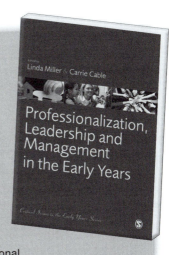

With the rapid change experienced by the early years workforce over recent times, this book considers what constitutes professionalization in the sector, and what this means in practice. Bringing a critical perspective to the developing knowledge and understanding of early years practitioners at various stages of their professional development, it draws attention to key themes and issues. Chapters are written by leading authorities, and case studies, questions and discussion points are provided to facilitate critical thinking.

Topics covered include:

- constructions of professional identities
- men in the early years
- multidisciplinary working in the early years
- professionalization in the nursery
- early childhood leadership and policy.

Written in an accessible style and relevant to all levels of early years courses, the book is highly relevant to those studying at masters level, and has staggered levels of further reading that encourage reflection and progression.

CRITICAL ISSUES IN THE EARLY YEARS

November 2010 • 184 pages
Cloth (978-1-84920-553-5) • £65.00
Paper (978-1-84920-554-2) • £22.99

ALSO FROM SAGE